The Library of Southern Civilization
Lewis P. Simpson, Editor

Carpetbagger
from Vermont

Captain Marshall Harvey Twitchell in the fall of 1864.
Courtesy of Dr. Marshall Coleman Twitchell.

Carpetbagger
from Vermont

The Autobiography of Marshall Harvey Twitchell

Edited, and with an introduction, by Ted Tunnell

Louisiana State University Press
Baton Rouge and London

Designer: Diane B. Didier
Typeface: Trump Mediaeval
Typesetter: G & S Typesetters, Inc.
Printer: Thomson-Shore, Inc.
Binder: John H. Dekker & Sons, Inc.

Library of Congress Cataloging-in-Publication Data
Twitchell, Marshall Harvey.
  Carpetbagger from Vermont : the autobiography of Marshall Harvey
Twitchell / edited and with an introduction by Ted Tunnell.
    p.   cm. — (Library of Southern civilization)
  Includes index.
  ISBN 0-8071-1415-4
  1. Twitchell, Marshall Harvey.   2. Reconstruction—Louisiana.
3. Louisiana—Politics and government—1865-1950.   4. Politicians—
Louisiana—Biography.   5. United States.   Bureau of Refugees,
Freedmen, and Abandoned Lands—Officials and employees—Biography.
I. Tunnell, Ted.   II. Title.   III. Series.
F375.T95 1989
976.3'06'0924—dc 19   88-8225
[B]   CIP

The paper in this book meets the guidelines for permanence and durability of the
Committee on Production Guidelines for Book Longevity of the Council on
Library Resources. ∞

For Letitia and my parents

Contents

Illustrations

Carpetbagger
from Vermont

Editor's Introduction

The year was 1861. Barely three months had passed since the Confederates fired on Fort Sumter and President Lincoln called for troops. The nation's capital on the Potomac River ordinarily dozed in the summertime heat, but during this first summer of the Civil War, Congress was in special session and Washington was a bustling military encampment. In the third week of July, the new Federal army left the safety of the capital and marched twenty miles into Virginia, colliding with the Rebels at Bull Run near Manassas Junction. The battle began well enough for the North but ended with the Union troops fleeing the field in defeat. Contrary to Northern hopes, the Southern rebellion would not be over by autumn after all.

On a small farm in the rugged hills of southern Vermont, twenty-one-year-old Marshall Harvey Twitchell followed the war news. The alarming reports of Bull Run persuaded him to enlist. He was a patriotic youth, and the war promised excitement and a chance to see New York, Philadelphia, Washington, and perhaps Richmond. Then, too, the family was poor, and the army may have seemed a ready escape from the hardscrabble existence and limited opportunities of Vermont's rocky hillsides. Young Twitchell's mother and three sisters tearfully pleaded with him to remain at home. His father, Harvey Daniel Twitchell, was uncharacteristically silent. On the appointed day, however, he offered to drive his son to the recruiting office in the nearby village of Jamaica, and during the journey he added his voice to those of his wife and daughters, urging the boy to stay home. The young man was adamant, and as he left the recruiter, he saw the first tears he had ever seen in his father's eyes. The sight evoked his first suspicion that putting down the rebellion in the South was not going to be the lark he imagined. How could he know that the short ride with his father was the beginning of a strange and terrible adventure, as poignant as any story in the savage annals of the Civil War and Reconstruction.

Twitchell was mustered into the 4th Vermont Regiment at Brattleboro in September. His regiment was one of the original units of the legendary Vermont Brigade; it suffered the highest casualties in the Union army, but it never lost a battle flag to the enemy. Through three years of hard campaigning, Twitchell escaped with only minor wounds, but his luck nearly ran out at the Wilderness in May, 1864, when he suffered a near-fatal head wound. He awoke one evening to find the Army of the Potomac moving out for Spotsylvania Courthouse and himself left behind in a tent for the dying. He resolved that though his tentmates might be goners, he was still very much alive. His head was grotesquely swollen, and he could barely see. Prying one eye open with his fingers, he stumbled out into the road and the next morning had the good fortune to be picked up by a Vermont ambulance train. He eventually made his way to Fredericksburg, thence to a Washington hospital, and finally home to Vermont for a long rest. He returned to command a company of the 109th Colored Troops at the siege of Petersburg.

Posted to Texas after the war, Twitchell requested reassignment to the Freedmen's Bureau in Louisiana. In the fall of 1865, he received orders from bureau headquarters in New Orleans sending him to the village of Sparta in Bienville Parish, a remote sector of the upper Red River valley. His half-year stint as a bureau agent was more or less routine, but his personal life began to take on the aura of a romantic novel. Adele Coleman was a pretty, young schoolteacher at Sparta Academy; her family was local gentry. Over the vehement objections of family and friends, Adele decided that the beau of her choice was the hated Yankee captain of the Freedmen's Bureau (Twitchell seems to have been the pursued party). Isaac Coleman attempted to send his headstrong teenage daughter to South Carolina, but she refused to go. For a time Adele's older brother Gus and Twitchell appeared on the verge of bloodshed. At length the family relented, and in July, 1866, Marshall and Adele were married in the Coleman home in Brush Valley.

The Colemans soon discovered a silver lining in the Yankee cloud that had drifted over their lives. The new son-in-law had saved his army pay and bounties and, more important, displayed business talent lacking in the Coleman men. In return for teaching him about planting cotton, the Louisianians received a thorough schooling in Yankee enterprise. Within two years Twitchell was acting as the business manager of the Coleman lands as well as running his own plantation. At a time when most Northern planters in the South were awash in failure, this exceptional New Englander thrived. Adele boasted proudly to her sister that her husband had done wonders in straightening out her father's affairs. "He has paid off all the land notes and $100 on the stock note, besides taking up an old note of Barrett's against Pa. Gus and Marshall has paid all [Pa's] debts in Ringgold. . . . I can say thank the Lord the plantation is paid for 'every cent' and there will be no trouble about the balance that Pa owes. Pa says he don't know what in the world he would have done without his *Yankee* son in law to help him out." She confided that she must live frugally for a time, because Marshall "has paid out all his money in paying Pa's debts but the day is not far distant when I can have any thing I want."[1]

Twitchell's newfound prosperity was a magnet for the rest of his family. During 1869 and 1870, his brother Homer, his three sisters and their husbands, and his mother—his father had died during the war—all moved from Vermont to Starlight Plantation, his new estate on the west bank of the Red River in De Soto Parish. The new arrivals helped manage his growing operations, which now included a steam-powered sawmill and grist-mill complex at Starlight. They also held political jobs, because their enterprising kinsman was active in politics.

The Reconstruction Acts had opened the gates of political opportunity to men like Twitchell all over the South. With the old elite temporarily disfranchised and the untutored former slaves in search of leadership, an able Northerner had easy access to public office. Twitchell embraced the Republican party and represented Bienville Parish in the state constitutional convention of 1867–

1. Lawrence N. Powell, *New Masters: Northern Planters During the Civil War and Reconstruction* (New Haven, 1980); Adele Twitchell to her sister Lou, January 30, 1869 (or possibly January 8, 1868), in Marshall Harvey Twitchell Papers, Prescott Memorial Library, Louisiana Tech University, Ruston.

1868. In 1871 he claimed a seat in the Louisiana senate and engineered the creation of Red River Parish, a political reorganization of the upper Red River region that consolidated his own and his party's strength. His influence soon extended far beyond the borders of his own bailiwick. The Louisiana Republican party depended on black voters, who lived mainly in the alluvial bottomlands of the Red River and the Mississippi. In contrast to the broad Mississippi lowlands, the floodplain of the Red River was narrow and flanked by uplands peopled with hostile whites. Republicans along the Red River, in other words, were vulnerable, and that vulnerability made Twitchell both an indispensable man and a target.

Louisiana whites nearly ousted the Republicans in the disputed election of 1872. When that effort failed they turned to terror. On Easter Sunday, 1873, a small army of whites murdered 105 black farmers at Colfax courthouse, about fifty miles south of Starlight. The following year angry whites formed the White League, the successor to the Knights of the White Camellia (the Louisiana version of the Ku Klux Klan). The White League started in the lower Red River valley in the spring and spread rapidly across the state. In July it overturned the parish government of Natchitoches, and the next month, while Twitchell was in New Orleans, it hit Red River Parish. Twitchell's brother Homer, the husbands of his sisters Kate and Belle, and three other Republicans were murdered in a grisly episode known as the Coushatta Massacre. In September the terrorists overran New Orleans. Had President Grant not intervened with federal troops, Reconstruction in the state would have collapsed that fall.

Twitchell's last years in Louisiana were grim almost beyond belief. On the morning of May 2, 1876, he left Starlight for a meeting of the police jury in nearby Coushatta, accompanied by his surviving brother-in-law, George King. As they prepared to disembark from the Red River ferry, a sinister figure with a repeating rifle appeared on the bank above. The assassin killed King instantly and fired six bullets into Twitchell, who survived only by playing dead in the water. Four of the wounds were in his arms, and to save his life the surgeon amputated both of them. In these mournful years his wife Adele and their newborn son, and his sisters Belle, Kate, and Helen all died of natural causes. Calamity piled upon calamity. After Reconstruction, whites in Red River Parish, using various pretexts, "legally" stripped him of Starlight and Briar Bend plantations. The story of the enterprising, self-made man climbing the ladder of fame and fortune had turned into haunting Greek tragedy.

In 1878 President Hayes appointed Twitchell the American consul in Kingston, Canada, a position he held for the rest of his life. After he was removed from the scene, the controversy surrounding his career in the South abated but did not disappear. It was kept alive by the legal battles over Starlight and Briar Bend, the investigations of hostile congressional committees, and a popular novel about a north Louisiana carpetbagger named Captain Marshall Witchell (obviously Twitchell).

Mrs. Mary Edwards Bryan was a prominent Gilded Age author and editor. A native of Florida, she lived for many years in north Louisiana. For a brief time after the war, she was co-editor of the Natchitoches *Times*. About 1868, she moved to a village outside Coushatta in Red River Parish, only a few miles from Starlight, where she remained during the years of Twitchell's ascendancy. The extent of her acquaintance with the Vermonter is speculative, but in so confined a locale, it seems reasonable to assume that they had at least met. In 1874, if not before, she left the parish and the state to pursue her literary career in Atlanta as a writer and editor for *Sunny South*, a regional literary magazine. Serialized in *Sunny South* and then appearing in hard cover in 1881, *Wild Work; The Story of the Red River Tragedy*, her second novel, is a fictional rendering of Twitchell's rise and fall. Almost sympathetically, Mrs. Bryan depicts her Yankee protagonist as a strong-willed, energetic man, marred by a tragic character flaw: lust for power. His obsession costs him his wife, his family, and finally his arms. Venality of the common sort, however, is alien to his nature. What is surprising, in view of her background, is the novelist's cold-eyed view of the Red River Redeemers. They are as power hungry as the carpetbagger they depose, and their White League is little more than a gang of assassins. When a later generation of southern writers turned to the history of Reconstruction for inspiration, Mrs. Bryan's work, blaming native terrorists as much as the carpetbaggers for the horrors of the period, was little imitated.[2]

2. James S. Patty, "A Woman Journalist in Reconstruction Louisiana: Mrs. Mary E. Bryan," *Louisiana Studies*, III (Spring, 1964), 75–82; *Dictionary of American Biography*, III, 190.

Twitchell had a good memory, and as the years passed he kept much of his personal correspondence and collected government documents and newspaper stories about his career. It was probably after the Spanish-American War, in which he had a small but unusual role, that work began on his autobiography. He finished the main body of the work in 1899 or 1900 and then added a few pages on the Boer War, the death of Queen Victoria, and other contemporary events in the spring of 1901.[3] The last page and a half (actually pasted in) concern a letter dated June 5, 1901, about his Civil War record. This entry must have been made within a few weeks of that date, because on July 10, Twitchell's cousin, Fred Felton Twitchell, purchased a typed copy of the complete manuscript. A handwritten note at the front of the cousin's copy throws a ray of light on Twitchell's plans for the work: "Sold to F F Twitchell of St Albans Vermont for his personal use but not with the right of publication which is reserved to M H Twitchell and his heirs."[4]

How Twitchell wrote the story is a matter of some importance. He had been fitted with primitive artificial arms and could actually scratch a zigzag signature. It seems impossible, however, that he could have manually typed a long manuscript when he could neither feed himself nor dress without assistance. He must have dictated the story, most likely to his son Emmus George, a clerk in the consulate. Dictation would help explain the document's distinctive style, because the cadence of Twitchell's prose appears to be that of a man talking rather than writing. This oral style may also help explain some of the organizational problems discussed in the following section, Editorial Problems and Practices.

The reputation of Reconstruction Republicans, never high since the 1870s, was in precipitous decline at the turn of the century. In 1899 Thomas Nelson Page's fictional indictment of Reconstruction, *Red Rock*, was a national best seller. The year Twitchell finished his manuscript, the Reverend Thomas Dixon began work

3. The typeface of these concluding pages is slightly smaller than that in the rest of the manuscript, and the titles of the post-1900 chapters were plainly added (in the same smaller typeface) to the table of contents after the original typing.

4. Regrettably, Twitchell did not correct or revise the autobiography before it was copied; except for the correction of some of the more obvious typographical errors and the addition of a brief line about Queen Victoria, the document was retyped verbatim, mistakes and all. This copy of the manuscript now belongs to Harry G. Twitchell of Greenwich, Connecticut.

on the Reconstruction trilogy that would leave an indelible image of Republican villainy in the popular imagination (especially after the second volume was made into the epic silent film *The Birth of a Nation*). In these years scholars of national rank, such as William Archibald Dunning and John W. Burgess, condemned Reconstruction as a tragic mistake.[5] Twitchell was painfully aware of the trend. "There is no part of the history of the United States," he predicted in his preface, "of which in a few years so little will be known as that portion which may be designated as the 'Reconstruction period' of the Southern states. There is no equal time of which so much was published that was false and so little that was true." Young Northerners like himself, so-called carpetbaggers, went South after the war and attempted to uproot a civilization based on slavery and plant the seeds of freedom, and in large measure they succeeded. But, alas, their names "have been covered with obloquy and they themselves lie in graves unknown and unhonored."

The tone of Twitchell's preface reinforces the idea that, initially at least, he planned to publish the work in defense of his record. "I have referred to my parentage, childhood, boyhood, army experience and long consular service after my life in the South," he explains, so "that my character may be the better understood. . . . It has always seemed to me very strange that the Northern people should so readily have believed their young men the infamous wretches which the South represented them to be, on the testimony of men reared under the demoralizing influence of slavery, traitors to their government for four years and then gamblers and barroom loafers." Other sections of the work also give the impression that the goal was publication. He recounts, for example, how in 1876 a hostile subcommittee of the United States House of Representatives investigated the murderous attack on himself and King and concluded (contrary to the evidence) that the assault was not politically inspired. At the same time, the committee aired a lengthy indictment of the Vermonter's conduct of affairs in Red River Parish, or as Twitchell aptly put it, the

---

5. The trilogy consists of *The Leopard's Spots* (New York, 1902), *The Clansman* (New York, 1905), and *The Traitor* (New York, 1907). See William Archibald Dunning, *Essays on the Civil War and Reconstruction* (New York, 1897), and *Reconstruction: Political and Economic* (New York, 1907); and John W. Burgess, *Reconstruction and the Constitution, 1866–1867* (New York, 1902).

committee proceeded "to try me for being shot." He takes up the committee's allegations point by point and refutes them at some length, for the most part quite effectively.

However openly they discussed their public acts, nineteenth-century memoirists usually drew a veil around their private lives. Twitchell was no exception, and his reticence about his family, especially the women, is yet another indicator that his original aim was publication. Apart from the dramatic events of their courtship, we learn next to nothing about his life with Adele Coleman and even less about his marriage to Henrietta Day. He wrote to defend his public life, not to parade his private affairs.

It is not hard to imagine why the aging carpetbagger never carried the project of publishing his memoirs to completion. Even for an experienced writer, the tedious labor of preparing a manuscript for publication can be a time-consuming and emotionally draining task. Twitchell plainly lacked expertise, and the long road to print would have been especially daunting because of his disability, which made him dependent on someone else for every correction and revision, no matter how minor. Henrietta's death in 1902 might also have undermined his enthusiasm for the project. Whatever the reason, after completing what was essentially a first draft, Twitchell abandoned the effort.

Excluding the introductory pages on his early life and the short closing chapters centered on the consulate at Kingston, Twitchell's narrative falls into two main parts. The first, and shorter, section tells about his Civil War experiences, of which he was very proud. While these pages contain little of significance for students of the military campaigns, those interested in the sorts of questions explored by Bell Irvin Wiley in *The Life of Billy Yank* and *The Life of Johnny Reb* will find them valuable. Of main interest to most readers, however, will be the long section on Reconstruction, where Twitchell gives an inside view of the rise and fall of the Republican party in the Red River valley. More than simply valuable, these pages contain material of unusual richness. The narrative is not only rich in political history; it also contains vivid descriptions of life and society in north Louisiana. Social historians will find much of value here.

In one respect, it is perhaps just as well that Twitchell never published his story. He was not a self-conscious man, and there is an unguarded quality about his writing that is rare in a published

work. Because it did not go to press, he never had to scrutinize
every line of text, asking himself, "How does this make me look
to my readers?" Possibly for this reason, his narrative is surpris-
ingly free of sanctimony. He reveals himself as a born intriguer
who was addicted to the danger and excitement of his life in Louisiana—the midnight rides, the hairbreadth escapes, the air of crisis, the stormy senate sessions. And when it was all over, despite
the terrible cost, he confesses that he missed it. The peace and
quiet of New England villages in the late 1870s taxed his patience,
and the slow routine of the consulate in Kingston was almost
more than he could bear.

Only a handful of Southern Republicans published books about
their Reconstruction experiences, and still fewer of these were
carpetbaggers. The best-known is Albion W. Tourgée, whose novel
A Fool's Errand is a period classic. If we exclude works of fiction,
the list of book-length carpetbagger memoirs shrinks to scarcely
more than four: Albert T. Morgan's *Yazoo; or On the Picket Line
of Freedom in the South*, Henry W. Warren's *Reminiscences of a
Mississippi Carpet-bagger*, Powell Clayton's *The Aftermath of
the Civil War, in Arkansas*, and Henry Clay Warmoth's *War, Politics and Reconstruction: Stormy Days in Louisiana*.

Twitchell's account readily invites comparison with that of his
fellow Louisianian, Governor Warmoth. Although both men were
former Union officers, in outlook and experience they were vastly
different. Reared in southern Illinois, Warmoth liked the South,
admired Southerners, and remained in Louisiana until his death
in 1931. Twitchell, an arrogant New England Yankee, was con-
temptuous of every aspect of Southern life and not a bit reluctant
to say so. In significant ways, however, their differences comple-
ment one another. The governor viewed Reconstruction from the
vantage point of metropolitan New Orleans, the state capital in
that era; the Vermonter observed events as the inhabitant of a
rural and isolated hinterland. Warmoth wrote mainly about the
first half of Radical Reconstruction (1868–1872), when he was
governor; Twitchell concentrated on the second half of the period
(1872–1877), when the Radical regime was overthrown. Considered in tandem, the two narratives give a rich carpetbagger per-
spective on events in a single Reconstruction state. Would that
we had such sources for the rest of the South.

For over half a century after his death, Twitchell's autobiography was known only to his descendants and a few family friends. The document became more widely known in the spring of 1965 through the efforts of Jimmy G. Shoalmire, a young graduate student at Louisiana Polytechnic Institute (now Louisiana Tech University). While researching a master's thesis on the Coushatta troubles, Shoalmire learned that Twitchell's grandson, Dr. Marshall Coleman Twitchell, was living in Burlington, Vermont. Contacting Dr. Twitchell by phone, Shoalmire asked him if his grandfather had left any papers. Dr. Twitchell and his wife Laura informed the caller that there were boxes of letters, a scrapbook, and a typescript autobiography over two hundred pages long. Shoalmire's elation is easily imagined. He went on to write a doctoral dissertation, "Carpetbagger Extraordinary: Marshall Harvey Twitchell, 1840–1905," at Mississippi State University. He had evidently planned to publish a biography of Twitchell, but unfortunately, Jimmy Shoalmire died tragically young of a heart attack without completing the project.

Several years ago I was teaching as a visiting assistant professor at Tulane University in New Orleans. My own book, *Crucible of Reconstruction: War, Radicalism, and Race in Louisiana, 1862–1877*, had just been accepted for publication by Louisiana State University Press. Thanks to Shoalmire and the Twitchell family, I had been able to use the Twitchell Papers and a photocopy of the autobiography, both located in the Prescott Memorial Library at Louisiana Tech. My last chapter was built around the carpetbagger's story. One evening in the winter of 1983, Dr. Marshall Coleman Twitchell, still living in Burlington but now retired, received another long-distance call from a stranger in Louisiana asking him about his grandfather. This book is the result of that conversation. To my great regret, Dr. Twitchell did not live to see his grandfather's work in print. He died in January, 1987, at the age of seventy-four.

Editorial Problems and Practices

The manuscript "Autobiography of Marshall Harvey Twitchell" comprises 245 legal-size typescript pages. With a typed narrative an editor starts with the advantage of knowing with certainty what words are on the page, knowledge often denied those who must struggle with sometimes illegible handwritten documents. Still, like every manuscript, this one presents its own special problems. Some parts of it are comparatively free of trouble spots, while others are replete with typographical errors, words marked out, omissions, confusing syntax, and murky organization.

The most bedeviling problem of the manuscript is its disorganization. In places it is so acute as to suggest that, rather than Twitchell simply digressing, his typist must have dropped notes or pages on the floor and then typed them in the wrong order. For this reason I have reorganized and combined a number of chapters in order to arrange events in thematic and chronological order, reducing the original thirty-four chapters to twenty-five. In several instances I have given chapters more descriptive or simply more readable titles, for example, "The Peninsula Campaign" instead of "Our first Campaign"; and "The Outbreak of the War" for "The Breaking out of the War."

Twitchell studded his history with numerous documents that, for the most part, blend into the narrative and serve to reinforce his contentions. In several instances, however, lengthy quotations only add to the work's organizational problems. In relating the death of his sister Helen in Indianapolis (the most glaring example), Twitchell devotes over twenty pages to verbatim newspaper coverage of the funeral orations. This material is tedious, poorly organized, and adds nothing to our knowledge about the carpetbagger or his family. Almost all of it has been cut. For similar reasons I have deleted six pages of newspaper quotations taken directly from General Philip Sheridan's 1875 report on the White League (readily available in the *Congressional Record*, 44th Congress, 1st Session, 422), two pages of quotes describing the memorial service in Kingston for Queen Victoria, and an extraneous passage from the Louisiana Black Code of 1865. Where documents are included, I have, with a single exception, located the original documents and used them in place of Twitchell's versions of them, which contain numerous errors. In several instances somewhat more of a document is included than in Twitchell's original manuscript, and by the same token, several documents have been slightly shortened. The deletions are marked with ellipses.

Either Twitchell or his typist had some peculiar notions about paragraph structure. A number of times the apparent topic sentence of a paragraph is separated from the main body of the paragraph. In other instances, the logical closing sentence of a paragraph is likewise left dangling freely. In still other places, ideas that logically form a single paragraph are broken up into single-sentence constructions. While generally adhering to the original paragraphing, I have combined these fractured paragraphs in the interest of coherence and readability. For the same reason, a number of disjointed paragraphs have been broken up.

Twitchell was good at orthography, and most of the autobiography's misspellings are obviously typos. Whatever their origins, I have silently corrected the spelling errors, but I have retained the frequent English spellings of words, which reflect his Canadian residence. The author's erratic capitalization and spelling of proper names, place names, and military titles, have been corrected and systematized. Words have also frequently been hyphenated or combined in accordance with modern usage: *white-haired man* for *white haired man*, *drillmaster* for *drill master*, and *carpetbagger* for *carpet-bagger*. In a similar vein, *holding over senators* has become *holdover Senators*.

I have modernized the narrative's erratic punctuation to improve clarity and readability. Minor alterations in syntax have also been made and lapses of verb tense have been corrected. With some regularity I have inserted explanatory or conjectural words in brackets. Occasionally I have taken the liberty of adding the articles *the* and *a* without brackets where they appear to have been left out. Here and there I have also silently removed a super-fluous word or phrase. While my goal has been to make the story as clear and readable as possible, I have constantly guarded against the impulse to try to clarify that which is inherently ambiguous or vague.

The original manuscript and a carbon copy remain in the hands of Mrs. Marshall Coleman Twitchell and Peggy Twitchell of Burlington, Vermont. The two documents are identical in every detail, typed on heavy paper, and faded; without laboratory tests it is impossible to be certain which is the original and which is the carbon. I prepared the version herein using clear photocopies of both documents as well as the original manuscripts, which were loaned to me for several months. Harry G. Twitchell also allowed me to examine the 1901 retyped copy for an extended period of time. Any student wishing to examine the original text may consult the photocopy in the Marshall Harvey Twitchell Papers, Prescott Memorial Library, Louisiana Tech University, Ruston.

Carpetbagger
from Vermont

The Autobiography of Marshall Harvey Twitchell

Preface

There is no part of the history of the United States of which in a few years so little will be known as that portion which may be designated as the "Reconstruction period" of the Southern states. There is no equal time of which so much was published that was false and so little that was true.

The collapse of the Confederacy left the Southern states without government. The negro[1] was loyal to the flag but ignorant and unaccustomed to self-government. The Unionists—persecuted by the Confederates, neglected by the Federals, and with no love for the negro—were not in sufficient numbers to form a government by themselves. The ex-Federal soldier, or carpetbagger, had the confidence of the negro and Unionist and the respect of the Confederate; but although brave, frank, and honest, they were all young men without experience in civil government. He [the carpetbagger] was especially fitted by his army training for organization, but with that training his love for the exact truth had been stimulated and strengthened; careful of his own statements, he was inclined to believe that others were equally correct. He could not comprehend that the politician in the South ignores all of the Ten Commandments if necessary for political success.

In this autobiography I have referred to my parentage, childhood, boyhood, army experience, and long consular service after my life in the South that my character may be the better understood. The vilification of every man engaged upon the Republican side in the Southern Reconstruction was general. I do not think

1. Because Twitchell was absolutely consistent in lowercasing *negro*, the word has been left as he wrote it.

that one escaped. Without exception they were all classed as bad men by the Southern newspapers, and the stories seem to have been believed by the larger portion of the Northern people. Lads of superior character from the best families of the North, soldiers with unexceptionable records for bravery and good conduct, according to Southern report, became at once the most infamous of the human family; then they returned to Northern society and were respected by the community in which they chanced to live. Remarkable demoralization and a wonderful return to the ways of respectability and truth which could have happened and been chronicled in no other place than Southern political society.

It has always seemed to me very strange that the Northern people should so readily have believed their young men the infamous wretches which the South represented them to be, on the testimony of men reared under the demoralizing influence of slavery, traitors to their government for four years and then gamblers and barroom loafers.

There were some Northern men in the South who were no credit to themselves or benefit to the country. Others, who became discouraged by the dangers and obstacles encountered and the neglect of their Northern friends, drowned their sorrows [and] destroyed their usefulness by intemperance. But the larger portion of these young men zealously worked for nearly ten years to substitute the civilization of freedom for that of slavery. To a much greater extent than is generally recognized, this was accomplished; but as in many other cases in the world's history, the names of the principal actors have been covered with obloquy, and they themselves lie in graves unknown and unhonored.

1

Ancestry and Early Boyhood

I was born in Townshend, Windham County, Vermont, February 29, 1840, descended on my father's side (according to Reverend A. Morse, A. M., genealogist) from one of the Spanish followers of William the Conquerer, a man of sufficient importance to receive his special grant of land, [and] on my mother's side (according to the researches of Amasa Scott) from an elder brother of Sir Walter Scott.[1] My parents moved to northern Vermont the next winter after my birth, and my earliest recollections of life are of the days when we lived in a log house in Averys Gore (now a part of Montgomery), Franklin County. There I spent seven years of my early boyhood, experiencing my full quota of the joys and sorrows of that period. My sisters Helen and Isabella and brother Homer were born there. The birth of my baby brother was a great event to me, materially magnified in my mind by permission from my parents to find him a name. Chief Justice Homer E. Royce,[2] then a young man, during his fishing expeditions into our neighborhood, had liberally contributed to my limited stock of hooks and lines until his name was inseparably connected in my mind with a full supply of fishing tackle. For this reason, rather than for his skill as a fisherman, I named my brother Homer. When I was nine years of age, my father, with a number of families from Vermont, moved to Bedford, Missisquoi County, Quebec, to engage in a manufacturing enterprise; our stay there was short, and in less than two years we had moved back to Townshend, Vermont. In this last

1. His parents were Harvey Daniel and Elizabeth Scott Twitchell. Extravagant claims of noble lineage are common in family genealogies.
2. State legislator, congressman, and chief justice of the Vermont Supreme Court from 1882 to 1890.

move my parents were actuated by the superior educational advantages of that seminary town.

I improved[3] the better facilities for education in that section for six months each year without change, attending Leland Seminary until the winter before my sixteenth birthday when I was engaged to teach one of the district schools for three months at a salary of twelve dollars per month. My success was considered good, but as I boarded at home and had continually the counsel of my parents, I do not look back to this year as one of much self-development. From this time I attended the seminary three months of each year, teaching school every winter.

My second school, [where I] taught the winter I was seventeen years of age in the town of Wardsboro, was a hard one and some distance from home. My first glance at the school, in which there were a number of boys older and larger than myself, convinced me that I could not rule the school by force. I felt ashamed to leave and, after a great deal of thought on the subject, decided that the only way for me to stay there through the term was to get the large boys divided in their opinion as to whether it would be a good thing for them to carry me out as had previously been their custom with many former teachers. This forced study of human nature proved of more value to me in after life than any other term of equal length. The Wardsboro school was the last one in which I found it necessary to keep any article in my desk for the punishment of scholars. Teaching school in the winter, working on the farm through the spring and summer, and attending the seminary in the fall constituted my life work until the outbreak of the Civil War.

It was during the last term spent at Leland Seminary that I learned my first lesson in the power of organization and became impressed with the fact that ability and general fitness for position are not always successful but, on the contrary, are easily put aside if organization is against them. This conclusion was forced upon me by the following event. Some of the scholars gained the disapprobation of the principal by taking a walk in the evening during study hours, for which they were reprimanded at chapel exercises. Although I was not one of the party, I sympathized with them and wrote an essay on the subject in rhyme which placed

3. Twitchell frequently used *improve* in the sense of "to make good use of."

me quite as much in disfavor as those who were in the walk. From this time until the close of term, there was quite a division in the school, and although there were no recognized leaders, the older and better scholars generally took sides with the teacher, the younger and more thoughtless class with me.

The closing exercises of the school we were able to control, but it did not occur to me nor probably to the principal or his party that the post of honor, the valedictorian, would be claimed by this young and wild party. I did not think there was a student among our number who was fitted for the position and therefore voted for one of the other party, which, being without organization, was divided upon different members of their own faction. The party to which I belonged voted in one solid phalanx for me, thus carrying the election. Surprised and chagrined, I attempted to resign, but my friends would not hear of it and seemed to be in such high glee at their success that I concluded to wait and consult the principal, who had never shown any bitterness towards me, notwithstanding the opposition which I gave his plans. The principal, Mr. [George Erastus] Lane, advised me to go on and do the best I could. I never studied harder than I did from that time until the close of the school; my valedictory was a perfect success.[4] The election taught me the value of organization; my success [taught me] the value of study and gave me confidence in my own power.

I had always attended the Congregational Church. The minister was one of the old school and a very good man; perhaps he could smile, but I never saw him. He was accustomed to read three long, dry sermons to us every Sunday, no variation in his voice, no gestures, nothing to disturb you if you chose to sleep. For some reason, about this time a change was made, and a young man by the name of Cushman[5] (a direct descendant of Robert Cushman who fitted out the *Mayflower*) came to take charge of the church. He was a very interesting speaker, and churchgoing became to me a matter of pleasure instead of duty.

He brought with him from Massachusetts a niece, Henrietta Day, who attended the seminary. The first day she appeared at chapel exercises we decided that she was the handsomest girl in

4. His subject was "Christianity: Its Effects upon Society," as listed in the *Catalogue of the Officers and Students of Leland Seminary* (Bellows Falls, Vt., 1860), 16.
5. The Reverend C. L. Cushman.

the seminary, and a number of us boys commenced laying plans to get an introduction. Her living at the minister's house was awfully unfortunate, as none of us dared to go there for any purpose whatever.

Fortunately, an "At Home" was given to which we were all invited. L[emuel] I. Winslow, afterwards Captain Winslow, and myself both believed that if we could only get an introduction we could carry off the flower of the school. We attended the "At Home" together, each one on the watch that the other should not get ahead of him. We soon saw Miss Day on the opposite side of the room conversing with my cousin. Both started to pay our respects to the cousin, thinking we could thus force an introduction. Winslow started first, politely moving around the crowd in the centre of the room; I roughly went through the crowd and reached them first, received an introduction, and took Miss Day for a promenade, so monopolizing her as to give no one else a chance. I little thought how important this young lady was to be in the future of my life.

In my father's house there were very few novels with which I could waste my time, weaken my memory, and destroy my taste for other books. Consequently, my desire for reading forced me to the use of histories, which under different circumstances I should have considered dry and uninteresting. The most interesting to me was the history of Napoleon Buonaparte. This I read until I was familiar with every recorded event of his life.

The winter I was nineteen years of age I was engaged to teach the Winhall school. There was a strong opposition against my employment, of which I had no previous knowledge. A portion of the district desired that the superintendent of the school should have the place. I rode up to Winhall on Saturday and was to be examined as to my qualifications on that night. Superintendent Gorden, my rival, was to make the examination. The schoolhouse was filled beyond its seating capacity, all the voters of the district being present. Mr. Gorden and myself were seated upon the platform and the examination commenced.

I was fresh from school, possessed with a good memory, and consequently the examination was not troublesome. After a thorough questioning in the history of the United States, for which I was prepared, he took up that of Buonaparte. Committeeman Hall protested that history outside of the United States was not required by law. Another speaker thought that it had better be allowed. In the discussion which followed I discovered the reasons for the large audience. I requested Mr. Hill to allow the examination to continue, giving Mr. Gorden all the latitude which he desired. I repeated page after page of the history of Buonaparte amid the cheers of my friends. To the credit of Mr. Gorden, I will say that he frankly recognized his defeat and was ever afterward my friend.

2

Outbreak of the War

Lincoln's election, inauguration, and the exciting events following were familiar to me from the public prints, although in common with many others, I did not think the result would be anything serious.

The Battle of Bull Run gave me my first impression that the Southern people entertained a higher regard for their institutions than they did for the Union. I decided to enlist immediately after this battle, our defeat giving me an excuse for doing so, together with the opportunity of visiting New York, Philadelphia, Baltimore, Washington, and Richmond at the expense of the government. Thinking the war would be of short duration, I intended to resume school and the study of law, which I had already commenced in the office of Judge Shafter in the spring.

My mother and sisters shed some bitter tears, which I expected, and mother was very much vexed because father would not interpose his authority and prevent me from going. This was rather a new thing in the family. Mother had always used her persuasion, father never; and I was a little surprised when he offered to drive me to the village to enlist. He improved the time industriously, however, in attempting to persuade or hire me to stay at home. After enlistment, on meeting my father I saw tears in his eyes for the first time in my life; more than anything else this impressed me with doubt as to whether I was going to have an agreeable picnic.

I enlisted August 26 at Jamaica, in a company which afterward became Company I of the 4th Vermont Regiment. This company was made up of young men from Townshend, Jamaica, and Wilmington. The drillmaster was from Derby Line, the few weeks'

drill which he had previously received being his only recommendation for the captaincy to which he was soon elected by the
company.[1]

We were mustered into the United States service at Brattleboro,
Vermont, by Lieutenant [George H.] Higbee on the 21st of September, 1861; E. H. Stoughton of Bellows Falls, a West Point graduate,
was appointed colonel by the governor.[2] We went into camp at
Brattleboro and received rations for the first time like soldiers.

I had determined to be a veteran at once and expressed no surprise at anything. We were very hungry for our first breakfast, and
when ordered to fall in, did so with alacrity and were marched to
one side of the camp. Two rough boards elevated from the ground
upon sticks served as the table; tin plates, a tin cup of coffee, and
a piece of bread and meat, this and no more constituted our morning meal.

I stood very straight waiting for orders; after a time somebody
said, "Cook, bring on the potatoes!" The reply was, "Hav'n't any."

"Bring on your butter for this bread!"

"Soldiers don't have butter."

"Where is the milk for this coffee?"

"You boys who are not weaned had better go home."

We thought we were learning pretty fast, but most of us ate a
fair breakfast; the cool morning air of Vermont in September is
quite an efficient appetizer.

When we reached the Brattleboro camp we found Sibley tents[3]
pitched for us, twenty persons being consigned to each tent. About
one-half the tent [floor] was covered with straw for our beds, and
one blanket was issued to each man; some were in doubt whether
the blanket was to go over or under us. It was the general opinion
that if we were pigs we needed no blankets but more straw; if
men, we wanted two blankets. But everyone was allowed to con-

1. The manuscript gives August 21 as the date of Twitchell's enlistment, but
his Compiled Military Service Record (Record Group 94, National Archives)
shows that it was August 26. The drillmaster was Captain Leonard A. Stearns.

2. Edwin H. Stoughton graduated seventeenth in the West Point class of 1859.
In 1862, he was promoted to brigadier general, the youngest general in the army at
the time, and given a brigade. His military career was wrecked in March, 1863, by
the Rebel Partisan Ranger John S. Mosby, who slipped into Stoughton's headquarters, which was surrounded by thousands of Union soldiers, and captured him
sleeping in his bed.

3. Large conical tents.

sider himself as he pleased; there was no increase of either blankets or straw. Our night's sleep was very good, convincing us how very useless were the almost numberless articles in our sleeping rooms at home.

For a few days we were very busy receiving arms and clothing. Everything was of the best quality; black hats, dark blue coats with brass buttons, and light blue pants gave us, as we thought, a very fine appearance.

We drilled for a few days, waiting meanwhile for our army shirts, upon receipt of which we were to be immediately sent to the front. The colonel insisted that everything pertaining to the civilian should be left in Brattleboro when his regiment moved. At last the shirts came and were distributed, each man receiving two. Orders were given from the colonel that one was to be put on and the other into our knapsack.

Upon examination, we were not surprised that they were late in coming and concluded that the three days we had been waiting for them the manufacturer had improved in making the collars, as they were just immense, while every other part of the garment was an emphatic abbreviation. It required more than a casual examination to determine which end up it was designed to be worn.

In a few days we left for Washington, our first halt being on Capitol Hill. Here our tents were soon pitched, and we called for our straw but were told we could have none as there was not enough for the horses.

Here Uncle Sam issued to us our first rations. A load of bacon sides was thrown out onto the ground at the commissary's tent, and a guard called to care for it until it was distributed. He was posted without orders and, upon being relieved, informed the relieving sentinels that he did not know whether he was posted there to keep the bacon from running away or to keep the boys from getting near enough to be bitten by the maggots. I am certain that no time during its existence had that meat been more lively. Complaint was made to the colonel, and the meat was condemned and removed. It was the first and the last time that the 4th Vermont refused its rations. We always kept all we had and got all we could. We received no more meat until the time that this bacon was issued for had expired.

In a few days we crossed Chain Bridge into Virginia and took position with the 2nd, 3rd, and 5th Vermont at Camp Advance.

We were soon joined by the 6th Vermont, thus forming the Vermont Brigade which afterwards became so famous.

While in camp here a cavalryman was killed in a skirmish. His body was brought in and nicely laid out on a platform in a wall tent, quite a contrast with what I was to see later on.

Soon after going into Virginia, Company I was ordered on picket. We were deployed just about dark. I remained with the captain some twenty rods in the rear of the centre of the line. The night was dark and still; about midnight, notice was received that an attempt to surprise some portion of the line was to be made. The captain went forward to caution renewed vigilance. I went to the right and rear with no special purpose, but my mind was filled with the warning just received. The light from the rising moon was just sufficient to cause me to see everything where I was and some things which were not visible. Over the brow of the hill I was certain that thirty or forty men were lying upon the ground. I hastened back to the captain and told him of my discovery. We crept to the top of the hill to investigate. I called his attention to the regular manner in which they were lying side by side. While standing up we could occasionally see one, which from its light color we decided could not be the dark blue coat of our uniform but must be the unsoiled light grey of Confederate officers.

We hastened back to the line; our right was quietly swung back and faced towards the sleeping Confederates. We then waited for the rising moon to give us the opportunity of surprising the surpriser. Never had Company I been so quiet; the captain felt very proud that he had made the movement without waking the sleepers. A half hour we waited, during which each man thought of his home and friends and what a conflict would take place when we advanced. The moon was up, the light as good as we could expect, everything looked strange and weird as only things can by moonlight, when we were ordered to advance.

We were soon in sight of the whole length of the line. I could hear the click of the rifle hammers as they were drawn back; but what sleepy fellows those Southerners were. We no longer made any attempt at keeping still. Our nerves were strung to such a tension that it would be a relief when the enemy sprang to their feet, but they never rose. We advanced a few rods further and found that they were certainly sleeping Southerners, but the Confederacy had no power to bring them to their feet. Our gallant advance had been made into the neighboring graveyard. The line at once resumed its former position with a mingled feeling of disgust at their fright and pleasure at escaping the conflict. This was known in the regiment as Captain Stearns's graveyard scare. I never laid any claim, or even spoke while in the service, of the important part to which I was entitled as the original discoverer of the sleeping enemy, or of planning with the captain the manner of attack.

The 2nd regiment was at the first battle of Bull Run. I visited them one day before they had changed their old smoothbores for rifles and found them amusing themselves loading their guns with blank cartridges, placing them upon the ground, pulling them off with a string, and betting on whose gun would recoil the farthest. I heard the colonel of another regiment engaged at Bull Run say that anyone could tell when his regiment fired a volley, for the men would all be lying on their backs. Arms were much different before the close of the war.

In a few weeks we moved on to Camp Griffin where I spent one of the darkest winters of my army life. I look back to this season with sorrow and dissatisfaction, not so much with myself, as with the fact that during this winter, while the men of the Army of the Potomac were being transformed from civilians to soldiers, the loss from sickness was unnecessarily large on account of our ignorance of army life and the care of the sick in camp. The officers knew no more about the requirements of camp life than the men. After they had performed for the company their necessary duties with the commissary [and] quartermaster and on the drill ground, they considered their work completed. They would have thought it an impertinence to have advised an intelligent man of the company about pitching his tent, packing his knapsack, or making his bed.

During the early part of the winter I tented with the captain, to whom a clerk was very near a necessity. I wrote a good many letters which were published in the papers over the captain's signature; carried on in his name and by his direction quite a correspondence, writing, I think, every letter for him to a lady in Canada near the Vermont line, which resulted in the marriage of the captain to the lady early in the spring of 1862. I was allowed to write these letters with no suggestions from the captain except that he wanted to marry her if he could. I hope he made her a good husband.

The first death in the company was that of Corporal [Thomas M.] Bailey. To bury him with military ceremonies was beyond the knowledge of anyone in the company. With the army regulations and Hardee's *Tactics*[4] I was required to study up the question. I felt much relieved when the ceremony was over.

About this time the captain had succeeded in destroying the "goody" record with which he had secured his election and had turned out to be one of the best poker players in the regiment. The first lieutenant was quite a different man, and being not at all companionable for the captain, they commenced to disagree and the lieutenant soon resigned.

The captain proposed to me that if I would allow him to instruct me in gambling and then play with him against the other officers of the regiment, he would furnish all the money, give me half of the profits, and get me appointed lieutenant. It was a tempting offer as I had been in the service long enough to discover the vast difference between the enlisted man and the officer. After two or three days I informed him that although I would like a commission, I could not pay the price; that it seemed to make no difference whether a man was a gambler or not in the army, but it would make a vast difference when he became a citizen. I left the captain's tent and went on duty as a private in the company.

The captain promised to recommend me to be corporal in place of Bailey, deceased, but he seemed never to be quite ready to do it, until I became suspicious that he was endeavoring to find some excuse for not fulfilling his promise. I had seen enough of him to know that his being under obligations to me for favors received would be much against me, that in fact, he had only a small stock of gratitude and honor. A very important letter was to be written for him; it was carefully drafted (he having excused me from duty one whole day for the purpose). I wrote, at the same time, my recommendation to be appointed corporal. He came in from afternoon drill, read and approved the letter, and told me to copy it at once upon the proper paper. I handed him my recommendation

4. William J. Hardee, *Rifle and Light Infantry Tactics* (2 vols.; Philadelphia, 1855).

and asked him to sign it. He was at once in a great rage, and it was not until after I told him I should not write his letter that he cooled down and signed it.

The colonel of the regiment placed among the calls a "sink call."[5] The company fell in and was marched to the sink, creating an immense amount of sport; its immensity can only be comprehended by an old soldier.

Near the close of winter occurred an incident which resulted in my being, for the only time while in the army, placed under arrest. As corporal, I was in charge of a small picket post on the main road towards Fairfax. Among the members of the squad was W[illiam] W. Pierce, afterwards Captain Pierce. I think it was he who persuaded me (I was easily persuaded) that it would be a good idea to go outside of the lines to a house where we had heard there was a lady who might sing for us. We passed up a gully so as to be out of sight of our own pickets and reached the house. Pierce, being the elder and a good-looking man, took the lead. The lady invited us into the parlor, raised the curtain of a window at the end of the house looking towards the enemy, and insisted that we should be seated near the piano where we had no view of the grounds. I attempted to change my position, to which she objected. Pierce was soon interested in her singing, but I began to be suspicious and could not understand why this rebel woman should be so kind to us, or why she should object to my sitting by the window. I stepped back out of the room and house, looked towards rebeldom, and saw rebel cavalry just appearing in sight. I called to Pierce, "Get out of there; rebel cavalry!" and ran down the road to my picket post. There was no time to take the gully in our homeward journey.

Unfortunately, the field officer of the day was in sight of the post, making his rounds; he asked me my orders about allowing men outside of the lines. I told him it was against orders; he said he saw two men running towards the post and wanted to know who they were. I told him that I was one; Pierce stepped forward and said he was the other. We were at once ordered to report to the officer commanding the main reserve under arrest. Fortunately,

5. Possibly this had something to do with washing or bathing; however, in the common military usage of the time, a sink was a latrine.

Captain Platt (afterwards lieutenant colonel)[6] was in charge of the reserve; he told us to say nothing but pretend we were sick and, when the pickets marched by the camp of our regiment, to fall out and go to our tents, and that when he reached General Smith's[7] headquarters, if he was not called upon for us, he would not report it. We never heard any more of this affair, and with the exception of a very few, the fact that we were put under arrest was never known. Thanks to my suspicion the rebel troop caught no Yankees that day. This was a very narrow escape for us. We had just received our promotions as corporals, and reduction to the ranks would have been the mildest punishment inflicted. Captain Platt, an officer of our own regiment, chancing to be in command of the main reserve of the pickets, saved us. We both resolved that hereafter we would obey orders.

Two weeks later, on this same line, my resolution was put to an awful test. W[illiam] H. Miles, a member of the company and a schoolmate, was earnestly put in my charge by his mother, she seeming to think that I might have some power to guide and protect her only child. We were on picket. I was detailed to stay at the main reserve, acting as sergeant major for the officer who sent out the reliefs. It was his duty to make the grand rounds of all the picket posts at midnight.

The night was very dark, windy, and stormy. The duty that night was very disagreeable and dangerous from the liability of the officer to lose his way, get outside the line, and be shot by his own pickets. Midnight came; the officer claimed to be sick and ordered me to make the grand rounds. When I reached the post where I expected to find Miles, I received no challenge. A flash of lightning revealed him a few feet in front of me, sitting down leaning against a stump, fast asleep. The penalty was death. It was my duty to take his gun, that being the conclusive evidence of the condition of the sentinel. I was so near that I could hear the regular breathing of the sleeping soldier. This was an awful condition, my promise to the lonely mother in Vermont on the one side, my

6. Twitchell probably had in mind Captain John E. Pratt of A Company and not Captain James H. Platt, Jr., of B Company; it was Pratt who became a lieutenant colonel.

7. Brigadier General, later Major General, William Farrar "Baldy" Smith, commander of Smith's Division, Army of the Potomac.

duty on the other. The perspiration oozed from my face. Slowly I reached out my hand to take his rifle and raised it a few inches when he came to his feet and called out, "Who comes there?" I jumped back out of his reach and answered, "Grand rounds," with the countersign. He replied, "Advance grand rounds and give the countersign." I at once accused him of sitting down. He said, "No, I was leaning against the stump." I said, "You were asleep." "No, the storm made such a noise that I could not hear you quickly." I passed on feeling very happy. Since the war I [have] met Miles, and he laughingly said, "Yes, I was sleeping soundly but I knew no one was going to get my gun, which was the conclusive proof, as it was tied to my boot strap."

3

The Peninsula Campaign

In March, 1862, we broke camp, bid farewell to our large tents, and started "on for Richmond." I thought, with many others, that in a few months the work would be finished and we should be returning home. On the march we spent two very unpleasant nights, the first from not knowing how to make arrangements for sleeping on the frozen ground, the second from not being able to make a fire out of green wood in a driving storm.

In two weeks we started for Fortress Monroe on transports from Alexandria, arriving there the day after the battle between the *Monitor* and the *Merrimac*. I saw here the largest gun I had ever seen and which furnished us one of those amusing incidents with which the disagreeable features of army life are flavored.

Jeff Gale of our company was remarkable for his credulity and his great desire to spread the news. The morning after our arrival Jeff had been properly charged, by someone who knew his weakness, and let loose; I noticed him coming towards my campfire with that peculiar walk and glowing face which denoted that Jeff had important news for the group. Excitedly he asked if we had heard the news. No, we had not. Well, "Lieutenant Tracy[1] is under arrest." What for? "For stealing a shell from the Lincoln gun." (Tracy was the smallest officer in the regiment, [and] Lincoln shells weighed 484 lbs.). Of course we laughed. Jeff in disgust said we need not laugh; it was so, for they had found it in his vest pocket. At this, the storm was so great that Jeff started off for a more appreciative audience.

While [we were] camping at Newport News, the *Merrimac*

1. Second Lieutenant William C. Tracy of K Company.

came out and threw a few shells at our camp. Theodore Graves, fearing that he would get no trophies of the war to carry home, secured a piece of one of these shells, which he carried up to the commencement of the Seven Days' fight in front of Richmond. Men of the regiment were all very anxious for a piece of a shell, but a little later their anxiety in that respect was completely reversed.

Early in April we commenced the march up the Peninsula. At Young's Mills we came in front of the enemy's earthworks and were placed in line across the field preparatory, as we supposed, to charge the works. A few shots were fired at our line, and one man in the brigade was hurt. Up to that time I had never been so badly frightened.

I heard there for the first time those peculiar phrases which after awhile became quite familiar to us; a woman told us that when "youens" came in sight, "weuns" jumped onto their "critters" and left.

During the first ten days we were in front of Yorktown, I looked over what was said to be a portion of the earthworks of revolutionary times, was impressed with the showy headquarters surroundings of McClellan, the beauty of the Curtis place,[2] and the disagreeable order that all slaves must be returned to their owners.

The enemy evacuated Yorktown, and we moved forward to the Warwick Creek line and on the 16th of April took part in that unnecessary sacrifice of human life known as the battle of Lee's Mills. While the regiment was in line in the morning, a shell passed over it just before the order was given to load. Men in the regiment who time and again had proved themselves upon the field to be the bravest of the brave were made so nervous from this first shell that it was with the greatest difficulty that they could keep their hands steady enough to empty the powder into the muzzles of their guns.

Four companies of our regiment commenced the fight by skirmishing down to the creek on the right; four companies including Company I moved out into the field and at a double-quick started for the dam which it was our intention to cross for the proposed

2. Major General George Brinton McClellan, the commander of the Army of the Potomac, made his headquarters at White House, a stately home belonging to Mary Custis Lee (Mrs. Robert E. Lee). "Little Mac" burned it when he abandoned the area.

capturing of the enemy's artillery. About the same time a larger force from the Vermont Brigade was crossing the creek below the dam. Upon our appearance in the open field, it at once became evident to the dullest mind that none of us would be able to reach the other side by way of the dam. We threw ourselves upon the ground, awaiting further orders. [Stephen B.] Niles of my company was shot dead by my side; this made my position so uncomfortable that I decided to go forward a few rods and get behind a large gatepost. Upon reaching my new position, to make my comrades believe that I had the courage which I discovered I did not possess, I fired from behind the post. A shower of bullets satisfied me that firing from there would require the greatest caution. I loaded and was just putting my head out to fire again when young Albert Pike, who had crawled up behind me, cried out that he was wounded; as I turned my head, a bullet grazed the post where my face had been, lifting the hair over my ear, and passed on. I thought that I would try the other side of the post, shifted my position, and putting my hand out, it was grazed by a bullet just enough to break the skin. I made no further attempt to be aggressive.

We soon received our order to get back to the woods. While crawling back, I was hit in the foot but not with sufficient force to break any bones or put me off duty. Captain [Henry B.] Atherton, Company C, who was in this charge with a plume on his hat, was severely wounded; his was the last plume that I ever saw upon the battlefield. The desire to be known upon the field by the enemy as an officer was afterwards ignored. In this affair, Vermont paid 192 men killed and wounded for a reputation for bravery which her soldiers never lost.

That night a detail was made to throw up earthworks in the open field where we had been. I was detailed and although quite lame, I was ashamed to plead disability, as it was understood to be a dangerous duty. While [we were] being divided off into reliefs, standing in the open field, I stepped back from the line a few feet and discovered one of our batteries. All had been cautioned to make no noise for fear of attracting the enemy's fire; consequently, when a gun of the battery threw its half-hour shell into the enemy's works from a few feet behind them, every man instantly went over the fence into the woods. Having seen the battery, I did not go and consequently secured a reputation for coolness and courage which I felt that I was very much in need of.

Two weeks of fatigue and picket duty followed the battle of Lee's Mills with a little picket firing to relieve the monotony. On the morning of May 5th we crossed the dam in pursuit of the enemy, who were again falling back. Early in the day we heard the firing at Williamsburg where they had been compelled from the rapidity of Hooker's[3] pursuit to stop and fight. Then commenced what afterwards was so many times our fortune, one of those rapid marches to reach the field of battle in time to save our forces from defeat by being outnumbered. We had all of us seen enough of war to know that the battlefield was not a desirable place, but still I think that each man did his best to reach the scene of action at the earliest possible moment.

Just as we came on, an effort was made by some staff officer to make the brigade march double-quick. We thought it was impossible and did not change our step. A band which had been halted where we were going in struck up "Yankee Doodle"; the regiment cheered and in answer to the music immediately took the double-quick. A few shells thrown at the band by the enemy stopped the music and caused us to forget our fatigue.

We moved to the front of Fort McGruder holding the centre of the line, while Hooker, Hancock,[4] and Kearny[5] did the fighting upon our right and left. It commenced raining just before dark. Nine o'clock roll call came, and as it would not do to light a candle for this purpose, I had an opportunity of showing my usefulness to the company by calling the roll for the orderly sergeant from memory. We were so worn out with our march that we slept soundly in the falling rain until near morning, when the water under us had reached a depth which could not be disregarded.

Almost from the time of my appointment as corporal, on account of the absence and sickness of sergeants, although a junior corporal, I had been kept on duty as sergeant.

Just after the battle of Williamsburg a detail was made from our regiment with orders to report to the surgeon of the hospital in the field for duty. I was in command of the detail and, marching to a large barn, halted my men and went in to report. At the side of

3. Brigadier General, later Major General, Joseph Hooker, commander of the 2nd Division, III Corps, Army of the Potomac.

4. Brigadier General, later Major General, Winfield Scott Hancock, commander of the 1st Brigade, 2nd Division, IV Corps, Army of the Potomac.

5. Brigadier General, later Major General, Philip Kearny, commander of the 3rd Division, III Corps, Army of the Potomac.

the door as I passed in I saw amputated limbs thrown together, reminding me of stove wood beside the farmhouse door. I reported to the surgeon and asked for instructions. He said, "Go into the field, bury the dead, and bring in the wounded." As I turned to go, he called me and said, "Do not bring in men who are about to die. Let them die there." I was so shocked with the heartless orders and mannerisms that I made up my mind that I would not do the duty. I marched the detail to the place for its work, gave my instructions to the corporal of the detail, and started for camp. I found the adjutant in his tent alone and told him what I had done, that I was willing to fight but would not work under the surgeon; he ignored my last remark, [and] told me to go to my tent, that I was sick.

I think it was the next day, as we moved on up the Peninsula, [that] I visited for a few moments one of the enemy's earthworks and was a good deal impressed with the quantity of blood which had been spilt there, as well as with the bravery of the men who had remained there so long. It did not occur to me then that a large portion of that blood was from the artillery horses instead of men.

From Williamsburg we moved up to the last line in front of Richmond and took position on the north bank of the Chickahominy. In our advance we made twenty miles one day. This we thought at the time something extraordinary; we then had a poor knowledge of our travelling powers or what would be done by us in the future. It was here that the "gray back"[6] joined the regiment and with the persistency of an old veteran stayed with us during the war.

Nothing of interest occurred until the battle of Fair Oaks, during which we were under arms but did not move. It was very trying to the nerves of young soldiers, listening for two days to the firing, watching the smoke of battle, and every moment expecting to be called in. I was so thoroughly impressed with the terrific contest that I believed by the time it was over I should have no need of money, so I spent what I had for sutler's stores, congratulating myself that I would put my money where no one could get it if I was killed.

Soon after the battle of Fair Oaks, we moved to the south bank

6. He refers to lice.

of the Chickahominy, taking position at Golding's Farm, and in so doing crowded so close upon the enemy's line that men were shot in camp by the sharpshooters. So often were we called out that a single shot from the picket line would wake us from a sound sleep, and quicker than orders could be given, we would be out, rifle in hand, ready for our place in the line. After investigating and the order came to lie down again, we were asleep almost as soon as we had touched the ground. Every little while, by night and day, the enemy would amuse themselves by throwing a few shells into our camp.

Here was issued to us for the first time some compressed, dried vegetables which after being prepared we termed "corduroy soup." One day while [we were] standing around the cook's fire, each with a cup of this soup in his hands, one of the enemy's shells exploded just over the group; from force of habit everyone threw himself flat upon the ground with that rapidity of action which must be seen to be believed; soup flew in all directions. No one was hurt, but the loss of the soup combined with the ridiculous position in which we found ourselves waiting for the next shell, which did not come, and in some instances the comical looks of the soup-covered soldiers, was a picture full of amusement.

During the nineteen days that we were in position south of the Chickahominy, a man without diarrhea seemed to be an exception. I was one of the exceptions, which I attributed to my drinking no water, always coffee or tea made of water which had been boiled.

After the first two weeks picket firing ceased by agreement, although we had but little confidence that the agreement would always be kept. I was in charge of a picket post in the open field, a small earthwork about two feet high in our front. It was very disagreeable lying there in the sun, so I called to the "Johnnies" and asked them if they would agree not to fire if we would. They answered yes. We all stood up, but after a few moments one of the rebels quickly raised his rifle while we as quickly went down behind our works. They laughed and asked if we could not trust their word. I told them that I was prepared to believe that traitors would do almost anything. This of course ended our truce for the day.

From the elevated position occupied by our regiment, we had a

fine view of Fitz-John Porter's[7] fight at Gaines's Mill. Some heavy
batteries in front of our camp gave Porter help by throwing shells
into Longstreet's[8] advancing lines.

Almost as an introduction to Porter's fight was our engagement
at Golding's Farm.[9] The enemy drove in our pickets, and our regiment and the 6th Vermont were sent forward to their support. We
were in line of battle just in the edge of the wood, with a wheat
field in our front over which the enemy attempted to advance. By
a happy formation of the ground our position was very strong, as
the edge of the wood was a full four feet below the field. There
could be but one result; the enemy was repulsed, while our loss
was very small. So general and severe was the fire of the enemy
that where I was standing, there was a continual shower of falling
bits of leaves cut from the trees above us by the enemy's fire, but
not a man of our company was wounded.

In this engagement, when everyone expected that the enemy
would soon get our range and their fire become destructive to men
instead of twigs and leaves, an officer who should have felt under
great obligation to me for what I had done for him kept me continually moving from one end of the line to the other, ostensibly
to carry orders, while he remained behind a large tree.[10]

After the battle was over, some of the men called my attention
to this fact and asked me what that officer wanted to get me killed
for. I knew he was bad but did not think until then that he was
mean enough to try to get me killed for the purpose of closing my
lips that I might not divulge secrets damaging to him, which he
knew I possessed.

Sunday morning, June 29th, McClellan commenced his famous
change of base to Harrison's Landing. Our regiment was quietly
withdrawn from camp but the tents left standing. A detail of
thirty men, of which I was second in command, was left to destroy hospital stores and then with knives to destroy the tents,
taking care that our movements of destruction should not attract

7. Brigadier General, later Major General, commander of the V Corps, Army of
the Potomac.
8. Major General, later Lieutenant General, James Longstreet, division commander of what would soon be called the Confederate Army of Northern Virginia.
9. Gaines's Mill and Golding's Farm, as well as later engagements described in
this chapter, were part of the Seven Days' Battles, June 25 to July 1, 1862.
10. This officer was presumably Captain Leonard A. Stearns.

the attention of the enemy. Among the hospital stores was a large quantity of whisky and brandy. I was placed upon the detail because it was well known that I never drank intoxicating liquors. At that time I did not even know the taste of it; consequently, the advantage which came to me from being on the detail was wholly due to my reputation for temperance.

I found in the hospital tent a man of my company who seemed to be waiting for an ambulance to move him. The surgeon evidently had considered him able to move himself. He said he could not carry his knapsack; in attempting to help him I was surprised at the weight, opened it, and found among other trophies and useless baggage, quite a large piece of shell which he had brought from Newport News. I lightened up his knapsack, put it on him, and started him out. About this time the enemy commenced dropping shells into the camp, which so invigorated the sick man that he made good his trip to Harrison's Landing. Soon after the commencement of the shelling, our detail was assembled and we started for the rear at a double-quick. This attracted the enemy's attention, and the shells dropped around us unpleasantly near and thick. The officer in charge dropped behind a stump, telling me that he was played out. As soon as I found myself in command of the detail, I deployed and very naturally stopped the enemy's firing, as they doubtless did not feel like wasting shell upon a skirmish line. Fortunately for me the last of these movements was in sight of the regiment, and I was at once promoted to sergeant and kept in command of the destruction detail during the day. At a hospital tent we emptied a large quantity of whisky on the ground. A corporal of the detail, unknown to me, filled his canteen with it. At Savage's Station we were behind the line during the fighting, destroying military stores. We destroyed a large number of new Enfield rifles which had never been unpacked and emptied barrels of sugar into the brook until the current was turned aside.

About dark we were ordered to the regiment and placed in a thick wood, our left connecting with no other troops. About nine p.m., I was directed to take eight good men from the company and find out what there was, if anything, in front of us.

Very quietly we moved through the thick wood, it seemed to me for half an hour. I was just about to return when I saw lights in our front. We moved forward and discovered that it was a regimental camp with the regiment evidently out; campfires were burning, cooks at work, camp guards in place and nearer to us a sentinel at the spring, who had evidently seen us before we saw him. I stepped a few paces forward and asked him what camp that was. He replied, "The 16th Georgia." I did not need anyone to tell me where the regiment was, nor that it was time for me to take my detail back. I assumed the duties of provost guard and authoritatively asked the sentinel why so many men were in camp when the regiment was out fighting. He said they were only the cooks and camp guard. I immediately brought my detail to a right shoulder shift and marched them back into the wood, when we at once abandoned the character of provost guard and started back to our regiment. I immediately reported to the colonel that a Confederate regiment, 16th Georgia, was in our front.

In a very short time we commenced our march for White Oak Swamp. During this night we suffered much for water. I heard the corporal, whose thirst was aggravated by the whisky he had drunk, offer $20 for a drink of water.

As we marched through White Oak Run we dipped and drank water so thick with mud and droppings from mules and horses that sucking it through our teeth, there was as much filth left in the cup as there was water which we had been able to drink.

Our brigade reached the high ground on the south of the run a little after daylight. Arms were at once stacked, and everyone dropped down by his gun to sleep. I think we must have slept until about noon, when we were awakened by the dropping of a shower of shells into our column. Involuntarily, arms were taken and all started for the narrow belt of woods in our rear. I do not remember about taking my gun; my first thought was, what is the order? I saw the captain running for the wood. I started in pursuit, overtook and quickly passed him, went through the wood, and after a few rods I saw a man of the 2nd Vermont with whom I was acquainted, behind a stump. It at once occurred to me that for a man who had a few days before been promoted because he did not get behind the stump, I was not doing the proper thing. I at once turned around, met Lieutenant [George H.] Amidon, and we were as active in helping to rally the 4th Vermont and make a stand in the woods as I had been a few minutes before in getting away from there.

Much quicker than one would naturally think, the brigade was in line in the edge of the wood, so chagrined for the manner in which they had left the field in front that it would have been with gratification [if] we should have observed the enemy advancing across the field that we might punish them for making us appear ridiculous to ourselves.

The major in his haste had left his sword and pistols. I, in common with many others, had left my knapsack. Permission was given me to go back and get it and also the major's accoutrements, which was successfully accomplished notwithstanding the continuous fire of the enemy's skirmishers.

In hurriedly taking position after the stampede, our regiment was on the extreme right. About three p.m., I was sent with a small detail of picked men into the woods to our right with instructions to go down White Oak Run two or three miles so as to be able to report if the enemy was crossing down there. We returned just before dark, had a weary tramp through the woods, and found nothing. It was marching by night and in line of battle, face to the rear, always fighting somewhere in hearing, for seven days and nights until Harrison's Landing was reached.

The day we reached the James River it was raining heavily and the mud was very deep. For seven days we had known no rest undisturbed, and everyone was perfectly exhausted and discouraged. We had just prepared to lie down as best we could with mud underfoot and rain overhead, when I was notified that what there was left of the company must go on picket.

There was a good deal of hard talking because there was nothing except the rear guard which was fit for picket duty. I know now that it was the superior material of which the Vermont troops were composed which caused the detail to be made from them. The preceding ten days had just about destroyed the discipline of McClellan's army, and patriotism of that kind for which the Green Mountains are noted could only be relied upon in this emergency.

The next day the sun came out bright and warm. The enemy made a demonstration against our picket just as I was thinking of what a thin weak line we had to meet an advance, and of the condition in which I left the army the night before. A large shell from our gunboat passed over our heads and exploded in the woods where the enemy was forming. A few of these monster shells, with their wonderfully demoralizing tendencies, caused the enemy to disappear.

I have always been positive about the day of the commencement of what was known as the Seven Days' fight, but after that time I neither knew the day of the week or month, [or] hardly whether an incident occurred during the day or night. There seemed to be for us no night; it was one long struggle to keep the enemy from breaking our line until the army and trains behind us had moved far enough to the rear so that we could again change our position nearer to the river.

I remember at one time that the enemy was pursuing us on a road to our left so closely that they passed completely to the rear of our right. Night compelled them to halt, and during its darkness we passed out so near to them that the noise of their camp was distinctly heard.

We found the captain at Harrison's Landing. He complained that he had been sick and immediately resigned and went home.

President Lincoln reviewed the troops. When in front of the colors of our regiment, the top of which had entirely been shot away, and the line reduced from 1,000 men to but a few hundred, he halted, uncovered his head, and the tears could be plainly seen coursing down his cheeks.

One night during the brightest moonlight, what was left of the band played, "Home, Sweet Home." I saw tears in the eyes of men whom up to that time I did not suppose could cry. General Brooks[11] stopped the music on account of its effect upon the men and ordered "Yankee Doodle" to be played instead.

When the army reached Harrison's Landing, worn out with fatigue and discouraged, combined with the heat of the hot midsummer Southern sun, to all of which might be added a good deal of homesickness, I think we were in the worst state of health that we had ever experienced. I remember one morning that a majority of the company were excused from duty by the surgeon, but rest, reinforcements, and discipline soon brought us again into fighting trim. After about six weeks, when we were beginning to expect a movement up the James River, orders came for us to move down the Peninsula and up to Alexandria for the defence of Washington.

11. Brigadier General William Thomas Harbaugh Brooks, commander of the Vermont Brigade, 2nd Division, VI Corps, Army of the Potomac.

4

Antietam Campaign, 1862

Up to this time I had worried a great deal for fear that somebody would make a mistake in directing the army's movements, but I had now reached the soldier stage of my existence and gave myself no trouble about what others did, confining myself strictly to carefully minding my own business.

We reached Alexandria and went into camp just out of the city on the Fairfax road, learned that Pope[1] was being driven back onto Washington and that McClellan was relieved. In common with the whole command, I felt that we would not be able to accomplish much without McClellan.

For days we heard Pope's guns coming nearer and nearer to us. We were continually under marching orders and finally moved towards Pope's army, which we reached just in time to act as rear guard after its defeat.[2] Never before had we moved just slow enough not to get into the battle. Although we refused to be called Pope's army, it did not prevent us from desiring to take part in the battles in which his men were engaged, almost within our sight. About its fighting, I do not think it made the slightest difference to our brigade who was in command of the army, brigade, regiment, or company.

A few days and we were in Maryland looking after Lee's army, with McClellan [back] in command. Just before entering Maryland I purchased a pair of horsehide boots with very long legs, the backs of which were so thick that it was a wonderment to me that

1. Major General John Pope was appointed commander of the short-lived Army of Virginia in June; he was relieved in September.
2. At the second battle of Bull Run, August 29 and 30, 1862.

they had not been used for the soles. I had no idea of the good purpose which that thick boot back was to serve.

As the 4th Regiment charged across the field for the rebel battery at Crampton's Pass, a piece of shell, first striking the fence, struck me on the calf of the leg with such force as to cut through the boot and give me a severe bruise. The blow was so heavy that I fell to the ground, supposing that my leg was broken. The regiment moved on, General Brooks closely following; as he reached me, he asked if I was wounded. Upon my answering in the affirmative, he replied, "That is too bad, but the boys are going to get the battery." I never heard that the general ever made any other sympathetic remark during his term of service.

I put my fingers into the hole in the boot but could find no blood; [I] began to move my leg and to my joy found it was not broken but only numb from the blow; the thick boot back had saved the leg. I was soon up with the company and amused myself that night with reading the letters in the rebel knapsacks which we had captured. They seemed so silly that ever after I made it a practice to burn my letters as soon as answered.

The following day we listened to the guns of the first day's battle at Antietam. The next, we moved for the battlefield, wading Antietam Creek I should think about three p.m. in order to make the last fight for the possession of the bloody cornfield. General Sumner's[3] corps had just been forced back, and I heard the old general say that his corps had been "fought to a frazzle" and could not be relied upon to support a charge. I shall never forget the impression which it made upon me as the old white-haired man pointed to the right of us, where his broken columns seemed to be forming.

In a few moments the historic charge of the Vermont Brigade at Antietam took place.[4] The dead and wounded men whom we passed over were greater in number than I remember seeing in any other charge we ever made. Our line was halted just beyond the cornfield, where a slight depression protected us from the enemy's fire so long as we remained close to the ground. We had to

3. Major General Edwin V. Sumner, commander of the II Corps, Army of the Potomac.
4. The attack recaptured the cornfield (the scene of some of the heaviest fighting of the entire war) and the nearby woods; it did not alter the overall course of the battle.

remove dead and wounded men to enable us to lie down in line. The sickening smell from the blood around us was too much for many weak stomachs.

Just before dark we heard the enemy charging upon our right; soon we could see their column nearly behind us, advancing towards a little clump of trees from which our batteries were throwing shell and canister with murderous results. But it was Jackson's[5] famous command, and closing the gap, it pressed forward until I feared the batteries would be reached. Quick came the queries, "Who are supporting the batteries?" and the reply, "The 20th New York." This was a German regiment which behaved badly at White Oak Swamp, and we had nicknamed them the "Flying Dutchmen." While we were cursing the officer who had placed the "Flying Dutchmen" in a place of such responsibility, they suddenly rose and fired into the face of the Confederate column; at once everything was obscured by smoke. [For] a few moments the roll of musketry [and] the thunder of artillery with the yells of the combatants were commingled, and we saw the broken Confederate column retiring to its own lines. As soon as opportunity offered, our men sought the 20th New York and informed them that we were through calling them the "Flying Dutchmen."

It was during this afternoon that General Brooks, commanding the Vermont Brigade, was slightly wounded in the mouth. One of the men asked him with apparent concern, "Are you wounded, General?" His reply was, "No, I have had a tooth pulled."

In front of us for half an hour there was a fierce artillery duel at very short range, under the direction on our side of "Baldy" Smith. The Confederate battery was so completely destroyed that it could not be removed until after dark. The next day when we advanced, the dead horses and men where it stood left the impression upon the minds of the unsophisticated that none of the battery except the guns escaped.

That night I was placed on picket, having charge of quite a distance of our front. Picket duty was only crawling on our hands and knees some fifteen rods to the front, there to watch and listen to the enemy while our main line slept. After all was quiet, I heard

5. Major General, later Lieutenant General, Thomas J. "Stonewall" Jackson, corps commander, Confederate Army of Northern Virginia.

in my front a peculiar call of a wounded rebel, which seemed to indicate from the words, which were always the same and repeated in the same manner, that his father was dead. I supposed that he must be delirious, but about midnight a couple of officers from my regiment came to me and said that they were going to crawl out to where that man was calling and bring him in. They cautioned me to notify the line so that they would not be fired upon when they came back. The next year when I was at home I joined the Masonic fraternity and this midnight expedition at Antietam was explained.

We expected a renewal of the struggle in the morning, but with daylight there came only one shot from the enemy's artillery, which was located so far in the rear of their line of the night before that we rightly judged they were in full retreat and that this was a parting salute from their rear guard. At the bank of the Potomac we captured quite a number of prisoners, and I was much surprised to find that they were in no way discouraged about the prospects of the Confederacy. We moved from the bank of the Potomac to Hagerstown, Maryland. Here General Brooks was appointed military governor of the town, and our regiment was camped just outside.

Our summer's work had been made up very largely of battles, skirmishes, and forced marches, and had left us almost without blankets, tents, shoes, or change of clothing. Our clothes were alive with the pest of the soldier in active campaign, difficult for us to get rid of from the fact that we had nothing to put on while we washed our soiled clothing in hot water. Some apparel, on account of our proximity to the city and the curiosity of feminine visitors, was necessary.

I remember playing a joke on an old sergeant of the company who had put up for himself a reasonably secluded tent. We knew that he had shut himself in it with his shirt off and was at work reducing the number of the inhabitants. To a party of ladies looking around the camp, some evil genius suggested that if they would look into yonder tent, they would see one which was considered the best arranged in camp. They of course pulled open the tent. I don't know who was the most surprised.

While in camp here I learned a lesson which I have never forgotten. Underclothing, blankets, and shoes, for which I was suffering, could be purchased, but I had no money. I have never since failed to have by me money enough for any such necessity and many a time have been much benefited by the precaution.

We received quite a number of recruits at Hagerstown, and I was relieved of all other duty to act as drillmaster. Many of the officers of our regiment, commissioned and noncommissioned, somewhat perhaps from the example of the colonel, were very profane. Some took the position that an officer who did not swear well could not make men obey him. My education in this respect had been neglected. Never having been accustomed to profanity, I did not like to hear it. Many of our recruits were fine men, enlisting from the purest of patriotism, willing to suffer or fight, but resenting brutal and profane epithets. My detail as drillmaster was the first recognition in my regiment that profanity was unnecessary to control men. It was here that I received my appointment as first sergeant of the company.

After about six weeks at Hagerstown we finally moved into Virginia with commanders changed. We halted early in December under Burnside,[6] at Fredericksburg on the Rappahannock.

On one of the last marches the day was very cold, with snow four inches deep; sick men were dying in the ambulances from cold and discomfort. At night when we halted, there was but little sleep for want of tents or, in fact, anything to shelter us from the inclemency of the weather. That night of suffering often returns to me in my dreams if perchance I happen to get uncovered and am cold.

6. Major General Ambrose Everett Burnside, who replaced McClellan as commander of the Army of the Potomac in November, 1862.

5

Campaigning with Burnside at Fredericksburg, 1862–1863

The 11th of December we broke camp and started for the first battle of Fredericksburg. Our corps crossed the pontoon bridges on the morning of the 12th, in a thick fog, and took position on the large plain below the city. During the 11th and 12th the fighting was almost entirely to our right.

On the 13th our regiment was put upon the skirmish line, which we considerably advanced. Just before the forward movement of the line, I was instructed by the captain to watch a certain man of the company who had always succeeded in keeping out of the battle and [was] ordered if he attempted to run to shoot him. While we were crossing a ditch, the man silently disappeared, very much to my chagrin and surprise. I looked in every direction for my man, but without success; this was more surprising to me because it was an open, level plain.

The excitement and danger of the skirmish line soon caused me to forget the missing man. The position occupied by our company was high and exposed, giving me such an opportunity of seeing the brilliant charge of Gibbon's[1] division as does not often occur. The division swept by our left in five lines of battle, its movement as uniform, regular, and precise as they would have been on dress parade. There was but little firing until the woods were nearly reached; then there was a long sheet of fire, the division gallantly struggling and advancing against it until all was obscured by the smoke.

This useless and grand charge is the most brilliant picture of the war which remains in my mind. During the following night

1. Brigadier General John Gibbon, commander of the 2nd Division, I Corps, Army of the Potomac.

we were withdrawn to the north bank of the Rappahannock. While on our skirmish line, a bullet passed over my left shoulder, cutting thirteen holes through my rubber blanket, which I was carrying. I felt well satisfied that I was no taller.[2]

My missing man had conveniently fallen into the ditch as we crossed it and turned up after the battle with the story of not being able to find his regiment after he got out.

For nearly forty days we were busy with the routine work of camp and the occasional excitement of picket duty on the banks of the Rappahannock. Although my position as orderly sergeant exempted me from going on picket, everything that occurred was repeated to me by the men when they returned, doubtless losing nothing by the repetition.

About the middle of January the preparations indicated that another movement of the army was to take place. The weather was fine, the army in good condition, and the roads frozen hard.

I think on the 20th of January, we commenced moving to the right and learned that the Vermont Brigade was to have the advance in crossing the river at Bank's Ford. As soon as the movement commenced, the temperature became much higher [and] rain commenced falling, with the result that upon the morning when we should have been putting down the pontoons, we were called upon, with long ropes attached to pontoon waggons, to pull them through the mud to the banks of the river. All day long we worked in the mud and falling rain, with the water over our shoes, at this unpleasant job. At night we camped or rested on an elevation of ground covered with a small second growth of wood, our clothing, arms, and accoutrements so covered with mud that their original color was hardly discernible. I do not think there was a man in the command who did not fully understand that if there was any fighting done, it must be done by men who had not acted as mules the day before.

We were not surprised to learn in the morning that the forward movement had been abandoned and that we were to return to camp, ending the famous "mud march" campaign of Burnside. The mud march doubtless put as many men in the hospital as a severe battle, while the destruction of mules must have exceeded that of a hard campaign.

2. He was five feet seven inches tall.

The defeat at the first battle of Fredericksburg, followed by this second failure, gave us a general feeling of discouragement, causing sickness and dissatisfaction with everybody, especially the commissary department. In the midst of this gloom the removal of Burnside and the appointment of Hooker was received with the greatest pleasure. We thought Burnside was brave but unfortunate and distrustful of some of his commanders in whom we had confidence. A change for the better took place at once in every respect; vegetables were issued to the army, imparting to every soldier the belief that the new general was looking out for his comfort, while one or two furloughs given to each company completed the satisfaction.

In our regiment it was intimated that the two soldiers who kept themselves and their equipment in the best shape would be selected [for furloughs]. I tented that winter with Sergeant [Jonathan B.] Webster, a man somewhat in years, with a large family at home. We agreed as tentmates wonderfully well. He was willing to do all the work about the tent, get the wood, and keep the fire, and I was willing he should. My name was announced as the sergeant from my company to have the furlough. I was so much surprised [and] in fact had thought very little about it.

Upon entering my tent hastily that day I found Webster reading a letter from home with the tears running down his face. I understood the trouble at once, stepped outside, and after a few moments' thought walked up to the captain's tent and resigned my right to a furlough in favor of Webster, giving as my reason that he had a wife and children who would wish to see him and that Hooker would doubtless give us so much fighting in the spring that a great many wives and children would become widows and orphans. Webster received his furlough, and it was the last time he ever saw his family, as he was killed at the battle of the Wilderness. I look back to the surrender of this furlough with more self-approval than to any act of my life.

It was during this winter that the snowball contest took place between the 26th New Jersey on one side and the 3rd and 4th Vermont on the other. ["Both regiments formed in line of battle, each officered by its line and field officers, the latter mounted. At the signal, the battle commenced; charges and counter-charges were made, prisoners were taken on either side, the air was filled with the white missiles, and stentorian cheers went up as one or other party gained an advantage. At length victory rested with the Vermonters, and the Jersey boys surrendered the field, defeated."][3]

The 26th New Jersey was a nine-month regiment assigned to our brigade, unaccustomed to camp life or the cooking of army rations, and in general, lacking the old soldiers' ability to shift for themselves. Some of our Vermonters told them that the reason they lived so poorly was because they did not know how to forage. What was stealing and wrong in civil life was foraging in army life. They learned their lesson well and quickly commenced stealing fresh meat from our brigade butchers. We caught a large dog, dressed and hung him up, and as we expected, the Jerseymen stole him that night for dressed mutton. We waited until we were certain that the dog was cooked and eaten and then informed them of the character of the stolen meat, giving them the additional lesson, which they never forgot, that foraging did not mean stealing from their own brigade. For the remaining week that this regiment was connected with our brigade, we made life miserable for them by barking whenever they appeared. When we moved out for the spring campaign and took the route march, any stray Jerseymen whom we saw were greeted with a chorus of barking imitative of all canine species from the smallest poodle to the largest St. Bernard.

3. George T. Stevens, *Three Years in the Sixth Corps* (New York, 1870), 183.

6

Chancellorsville Campaign, 1863

Early in April, preparatory orders for the spring campaign were given, although we did not break camp until the 28th. There was quite a change in our orders and preparations; we started with five days' rations in our knapsacks and three in our haversacks. These and plenty of ammunition seemed to be Hooker's idea of filling all our requirements.

The baggage trains were shortened, but as this affected the officers more than the men, the latter were pleased, as they always like to see a fair division of discomforts. Hooker disappeared from our sight so quietly, with all of the army except the 1st and 6th Corps, that he was hardly missed by us when we learned that he was across the river waiting for Lee to retreat or attack him. Our corps and a portion of the 1st had crossed the river, expecting that the enemy would abandon the heights on account of Hooker's position in their rear.

On the 3rd day of May, we discovered what our actual work was to be. The 1st Corps, after marching around a hill the night before for the purpose of deceiving the enemy, had been sent to Hooker, and we were formed in three columns (Howe's division)[1] for charging the works on Marye's Heights. While we were throwing off our knapsacks and preparing to charge the same works over the same ground where the right wing of our army had been so disastrously defeated the December before, I could not help wishing that I could honorably be somewhere else.

Both officers and men understood the importance of moving with rapidity and so fast did we advance that the enemy's artillery

1. Brigadier General Albion Parris Howe, commander of the 2nd Division, VI Corps, Army of the Potomac.

(so far as I remember) did us no damage, the shots all passing over us to the place where we were about the time the guns were sighted. We felt that in running towards the enemy in that instance, we were running for our lives. Within thirty minutes from the time we started, we had passed over our New Jersey regiment and captured the heights. The other columns were equally successful, although I think at a greater cost. Brooks's division now took the advance until checked by the enemy at Salem Church.

We camped in line of battle that night below the church, with Fredericksburg and Marye's Heights behind us. Early in the morning while I was washing my face at a little stream not far from our line, in company with others, a solid shot fell in the muddy brook near us. I well remember the look on Sergeant [Marshall A.] White's face as it buried itself close by him; it fully expressed the surprise which we all felt, as the shot came from behind us. We were not long in learning that the heights in our rear had, during the night, been occupied by the enemy. The Salem Church fight had developed the fact that Lee was not going to retreat, and if we got back to the north bank of the Rappahannock, it would not be by way of Fredericksburg or any other point on account of the weakness of our enemy.

I remember this day as one in which I should not have been surprised at the enemy's appearance in any direction; we were continually shifting our position. The firing seemed to be at almost all points of the compass.

I knew that this fighting was but the prelude of a grand assault which would take place at some point for the purpose of breaking through and cutting us off from the river. I do not think there was a man in the brigade who did not fully understand the danger of our position, or one who for a moment thought our line could be broken. About four p.m., the rumor came along the line that we had just been reinforced by two corps. I turned with surprise to Captain Lillie[2] and asked him what two corps could possibly reach us. He laughed and in a low tone said, "Two pioneer corps" (about 20 men).[3] I saw it was apprehended we were soon to have such fighting that it would be best for the men to believe that they had been reinforced by an overwhelming number of troops.

We were shifted around until our regiment was well advanced

2. Captain Daniel Lillie, commander of I Company, 4th Vermont Regiment.
3. A pioneer corps was a small work detail.

and concealed by the thick wood in our front. The assault commenced. The troops on our right were forced back, and a heavy mass of Confederates came crowding forward toward the front of the 2nd Vermont, evidently not observing us; when [the Confederates were] within a few feet of the 2nd, it rose and fired into the enemy's face.

I do not remember that we received any order to fire, but a part of the old Vermont Brigade could not be kept quiet while the other portion was in danger. We poured volley after volley into the enemy's column until those who could walk had disappeared. In a few minutes, another column appeared upon our left. General Howe sent an aide to Colonel Stoughton, asking him if he could move his regiment back under fire. Stoughton replied that he could move his regiment anywhere and immediately gave the order, "Battalion right about march." A few rods to the rear, we halted and faced about.

I always thought it was strange that General Howe did not know that our brigade could be as easily handled on the field under fire as on parade. It was composed of men who enlisted to fight; parades were not particularly to their taste, and the soldiers did not recognize their necessity as they did the fighting. One man of our company was shot in the back of the neck while we were marching to the rear.

Immediately after this our company and E Company under Captain Lillie were deployed as skirmishers and sent forward after the enemy whom we, in company with the 2nd Vermont, had repulsed. We moved through the woods into the open field beyond. The right of our company, of which I was in command, soon came in contact with the rebel line of battle. We halted and looked to the rear, expecting to see our own line advancing; nothing was in sight. Sergeant [Horace] Blakesley came running toward me, saying the order was "Forward." To the left I could see Captain Lillie evidently waiting for me. In front was the enemy's line of battle. To advance meant death. Stepping forward to the skirmish line with the men, I gave the order, "Forward." As we reached the top of the hill, we received a volley from the enemy which, although seeming to pass all around us, did not hit a man. Glancing again to the left, I saw Sergeant Pierce running toward me calling out, "Left flank." Blakesley had lost his head and brought the wrong order. We quickly moved to the left, out of the enemy's fire.

During this movement Nathan Mann fell but immediately

picked himself up and started for the rear. I asked him what was the matter. He said he was hit in the eagle (the brass plate on the belt of his cartridge box). He agreed with me that the eagle could wait until the battle was over before receiving medical attention and by my orders returned to his place.

It was dark when the companies were formed and we started back to our regiment. On reaching the place, we found a line of battle facing and firing the other way. The enemy's line had slid in behind us while we were on the skirmish line. I proposed to Captain Lillie to quickly bring the two companies into line and fire into the enemy's backs, saying that firing in their backs in the dark would stampede any men. The captain replied that it was his duty to get the two companies back to the regiment if possible, so we quietly marched around their left and, about eleven p.m., reached our regiment.

The next morning in a thick fog we crossed to the north bank of the Rappahannock, and Lee's attempt to crush the 6th Corps, through the bravery of the Vermont Brigade, had been foiled, with greater damage to him than to us. As an incident of this conflict I have heard it stated repeatedly, without contradiction, that when the last assault of the enemy was about to take place, Sedgwick[4] and Howe were of the opinion that the Vermont Brigade could not possibly stop the enemy and that it would be better to place the artillery in front, withdraw the men, and by sacrificing the artillery, save the remainder of the corps. General Brooks opposed the plan, saying that he had trained those boys and the brigade could not be broken.

As we crossed the river, we halted almost immediately upon its bank and, under shelter of the little pines, dropped down to sleep. It seemed to me that I was only allowed to fall asleep when I was aroused by the sergeant major and told to make a guard detail. I found most of the men asleep; but one circle, with a rubber blanket spread upon the ground, was earnestly engaged in a game of poker, the blanket being covered with their cards and money. While watching them and wishing it was their turn to go on duty, a shot or shell buried itself in the ground under the blanket, covering it with dirt, scattering gamblers, cards, and money. The game

4. Major General John Sedgwick, commander of the VI Corps, Army of the Potomac.

was not resumed, the players remarking that Lee held too heavy a hand for them to play against.

Directly we moved back from the river and in a couple of days to the extreme left of the Army of the Potomac. For nearly, if not quite, thirty days, with pleasant weather, plenty of rations, and the comforts of camp, we enjoyed ourselves without thinking of the unpleasant things of the past or worrying in the least about the future.

7

Gettysburg Campaign, 1863

Early in June our pleasures were abandoned, and we started into the Gettysburg campaign. On Friday the 5th we moved down the bank of the river, our brigade in advance, and for the third time, in the face of the enemy, crossed over the plains below Fredericksburg. The rebel picket line was gallantly captured by the 5th Vermont, crossing in pontoon boats. Nearly all day Saturday our brigade was skirmishing with the Confederates, all the time fighting superior numbers. Saturday afternoon another brigade crossed over, and we commenced entrenching and strengthening our position against the enemy's attack. We entrenched, skirmished, and wondered why more men were not sent to our assistance.

June 13th, after dark, we started in a drizzling rain back across the river and towards Washington. The roads, as usual, were not used by us, but we were marched through fields from which small trees had been cut precisely the right distance from the ground for the stumps to serve as obstacles for us to trip over. We were very tired, sleepy, and cross; but as some comrade was always falling, or picking himself up with many varied expressions, the amusement was so great that I do not look back to that night's march with unpleasant thoughts.

All the next day we rested and waited for the baggage train to pass us. Just as we were thinking of going to sleep, the order came for us to move. All night and until three p.m. the next day we marched for Dumfries. This was one of our hardest marches on account of our condition, the rapidity of the march, combined with clouds of dust and excessive heat. When we halted there were but twelve men to answer to my roll call. I was one of the two or three who were able to build a fire and make a little coffee for the rest. I thought at the time that my father and mother knew but very little of the hardy stuff of which I was made when they calculated I should be sent home early from the army as too weakly and puny to endure its hardships.

June 27th we crossed the Potomac at Edward's Ferry and camped on Northern soil. It was not generally known that Lee was invading the North, and we felt that there was to be some severe fighting whenever we could catch him, the belief being generally positive that we could whip him if we had him out of Virginia, where he and his men seemed to know every foot of ground and where every citizen was a spy.

We had mostly thrown away our clothing, so that to change was impossible, and the pest of army life was making us very uncomfortable again. To dip our clothes into boiling water was the only remedy, so a large kettle was borrowed, filled with water, a fire built, and soon we were dipping our clothing into it, putting them on, and standing in the sun to dry.

I remember among many other amusing incidents the comical sight of one of our men who always relieved himself of immense volumes of profanity and tobacco juice whenever anything went wrong. The boiling water had shrunk his woolen shirt. He attempted to put it on, but it was so hot that he concluded to take it off again; it started but stuck with his head covered. He swallowed his tobacco juice and then found he could not swear until helped out of his position by his laughing comrades.

The 2nd Vermont Brigade passed by us at Edward's Ferry, and as they filed by us, we remarked what large, fine men they were, and wished that in the next engagement we might fight side by side with them, fearing that without our example they might not do as well as they could.

After the halt at the ferry there was nothing for us but continuous and hard marches until the 30th of June, when we stopped at Manchester on the extreme right of the Army of the Potomac, over thirty miles from the soon-to-be-famous field of Gettysburg.

The next day, July 1, we lounged around the trees, taking a much-needed rest, and wondered how much longer the horses of the mounted officers could stand our marches, as it was observable to all that they were much nearer the end of their endurance than we were. Near night it was frequently remarked that toward the west the cavalry had evidently found the enemy, as firing could be distinctly heard.

Just before dark the bugles sounded, our rest was broken, and the Vermont Brigade was marched past the corps, placed in front on the road to Gettysburg in obedience to Sedgwick's famous order to "put the Vermonters ahead and keep the corps well closed up." I do not remember any long halts until we reached the field of Gettysburg about two p.m., July 2.

All the morning of the 2nd, under a hot southern sun, hurried on by the firing in our front, encouraged by the ladies as we passed, and soon the necessity for haste made more apparent by the wounded struggling to the rear—we marched forward to the great struggle.

When we learned that the 1st Corps had been so badly handled and that their commander, General Reynolds,[1] had been killed, the feeling was universal that the anticipated great battle was before us. As we came near the field, we learned that with our arrival the concentration of the army would be complete.

Quite a number fell from exhaustion and sunstroke, but the fear of having his comrades call out as they passed him, "Cannon fever," kept every man on his feet until his senses left him. As we threw ourselves on the ground for a few moments' rest after our arrival on the field, seeing nothing in reserve but artillery, we knew that our coming was none too soon. In a few minutes Neill's[2] brigade was sent to the right, and we were marched up toward the center and finally off to the extreme left of the army.

While getting into position, we met a few prisoners, evidently just captured. One of them remarked as they saw our white cross,[3] "Why, here is the 6th Corps. We left you fellows up at Manchester." Some of the men replied, "Yes, but after breakfast we thought we would come down and see what you were doing," while others volunteered the statement "that if we had known we were needed, we would have just walked down last evening after tea."

The position to which we were assigned, to the left of Little

1. Major General John F. Reynolds.
2. Brigadier General Thomas Hewson Neill, commander of the 3rd Brigade, 2nd Division, VI Corps, Army of the Potomac.
3. The insignia of the 2nd Division, VI Corps, Army of the Potomac.

Round Top, was one of great importance. Meade[4] was in great fear that an attempt would be made to turn his left, and I have since learned from conversation with General Longstreet that it was his earnest desire to make the charge upon our left which was made upon our centre.

On the morning of the 3rd, for the only time in my life, I saw a cavalry charge in our front. Soon after, a woman riding bareback passed through our lines to the rear. All day we lay in line of battle, amusing ourselves as best we could while the battle was raging to our right. The heavy cannonading which preceded Pickett's[5] charge we all understood was but the forerunner of close fighting.

One of the Pikes[6] of our company, in a scuffle, broke his wrist. It was very annoying to everyone that a man should be put off duty at such a time for foolishness.

There was great rejoicing in the brigade over the splendid behavior of the 2nd Vermont Brigade. It was considered of more importance to us than the result of the battle.

On the 4th of July, Sunday, with the rain falling in torrents, we were deployed as skirmishers and sent through the woods to the front to find the enemy. We found him behind a stone wall. He soon convinced us that there were too many of them for a skirmish line to drive out. I was in command of the right wing of our company, which was the extreme right of the skirmish line; but upon the enemy showing strength, I received orders to assemble on the left group preparatory to returning to camp.

The Confederates were so troublesome that to give the order as I received it would result in loss of men from the right of the line, who were quite near them and very much exposed; so I gave the order to fall back, covering themselves behind the trees. This movement naturally took more time. Captain Lillie, commanding I and E [companies], became impatient, waiting in the rain for my command, and called out, "What is that fool doing with his company?" I kept my mouth closed from discipline, but others of my number were very outspoken in their disapprobation of the captain's remark. In all my army service I had never before been

4. Major General George Gordon Meade, commander of the Army of the Potomac.
5. Confederate Major General George Edward Pickett.
6. At this time, there were three soldiers named Pike in the company.

called or spoken of as either a coward or a fool, and as soon as we broke ranks, I started for the captain's tent. He met me, pulled me into the tent, and talked so fast that I had no opportunity to say a word. He said, "You know well that I did not mean anything I said, and laying it up against me would only be an injury to both of us and no possible good to anyone." After a few moments' talk I concluded that he was right. We shook hands and [I] returned to my tent.

The next morning, July 5, we moved forward in pursuit of Lee's retreating army. As we passed over the field, we came in contact with the after horrors of the battlefield, unpleasant and unnerving to the recruit, but to us it had become too common a scene to cause much nervousness. Unburied and hastily buried dead, scattered accoutrements, and dead horses were to be seen in every direction. But when we reached the rear of the field and saw the immense number of wounded filling every barn and hundreds of tents, it seemed to the unsophisticated as though but little of Lee's army had escaped. I often noticed that the rebels were very willing to abandon their wounded to our care.

Before night we came in contact with Lee's rear guard, so strongly posted in a mountain gap that General Sedgwick halted and asked for orders before assaulting. General Meade decided upon a different course; we were withdrawn and the night of the 7th passed over Catoctin Mountain, one of those flanking movements in which marching took the place of fighting. The passage of Catoctin Mountain was one of the important events of my army life. The rain was falling in torrents; the night was so intensely dark that objects were felt before they were seen. The road or path winding up over the mountain was narrow and very rough, while the unseen obstacles in our way gave to the march that halting style so common to night marches. Occasionally, the monotony of the march was varied by some comrade getting too near the edge and tumbling down the mountain. To go down the mountain in that darkness and rain was out of the question. So, tired, sleepy, wet, and hungry, we halted for daylight. Corporal [Lorenzo] Harris and myself succeeded in finding four rails, placing one upon the ground [and] the other three crossways on top of it, just far enough apart so that we could lie down upon them without going through to the ground. We straightened ourselves upon the rails and spread our rubber blankets over us [and], regardless of the falling rain [and] our hard bed, slept until daylight.

I was agreeably surprised the next day to find that none of those unfortunates [who had fallen in the darkness] had been seriously injured. Going down the mountain, tumbling over each other, and by the exercise warming up our wet clothing was quite an agreeable change from the night before.

We halted in a pretty wood at the foot of the mountain to make coffee and put ourselves and accoutrements in soldierly order. We had been long upon the campaign and from forced marches had become so reduced in clothing that the garments which we had on seemed almost alive with that pest of the soldier in active warfare. Unfortunately for us we had neither time nor conveniences for doing more than to try and diminish their number by what the boys called skirmishing.

A few days later, on the 10th of July, occurred the engagement at Funkstown. We went in with the belief that we were supporting Buford's[7] cavalry, but it immediately withdrew and left our single brigade to finish the fight which they had commenced and for which they asked help to continue. Here, in a double skirmish line, we three times repulsed the enemy's assaults in line of battle. Our position was most favorable, every man being protected by a tree in his front, while the rebels had to advance through open fields.

It was in this engagement that Henry Bellemy, a classmate of mine at Leland Seminary, was killed. I presume he thought, as he was a recruit, that he must expose himself more than the old men so as to establish a reputation for bravery; it cost him his life.

It was here that Captain Lillie used Nathan Mann to distribute ammunition from tree to tree, saying in an undertone to me, "Somebody must do it, and Nathan is no loss to the company if he gets killed." Nathan did not get killed, nor was the duty unpleasant to him, as he had not sense enough to know that he was in danger.

For the ten days following the battle of Funkstown, we were marching and countermarching in pursuit of Lee, until we finally halted for rest near Warrington, Virginia. Our company at this

7. Major General John Buford, commander of the 1st Cavalry Division, Army of the Potomac.

time was almost destitute of clothing and shoes and from continual marches and fighting with an unchanged diet of hard bread and salt pork—much of the time on short rations, drinking from the muddy brooks as we passed through them—was in such a poor state of health that a man without diarrhea was almost a curiosity.

The fields around Warrington were covered with running blackberries. The surgeon excused men from duty and ordered them to go and eat these berries. In some cases I drove men out of their tents into the blackberry fields for that purpose; they felt so weak that only under the inexorable military order would they move. When a few days later we broke camp at Warrington, one would hardly have known the company; blackberries and rest had put new life into the men.

After some moving and shifting around, we finally went into camp in a beautiful grove near the banks of the Rapidan. We commenced to clean up and beautify the place, hoping and expecting to remain there during the hot weather or until we had entirely recovered from the Gettysburg campaign and [were] in good condition for vigorous work in the fall.

Very unexpectedly we received orders upon the 10th of August to turn in our quartermaster stores and be ready to march to the railroad station. This indicated to us that our movement was for more than an ordinary distance, and as we all knew what our record was in the army, we presumed we were to engage in some important and desperate undertaking which would result in glory and promotion for those who survived.

8

Enforcing the Draft in New York City, 1863

The secret as to our place of destination was kept from us much longer than usual. When we found out we were going to New York City to enforce the draft,[1] there was a combined feeling in the brigade of anger, disappointment, and pleasure, just as each man happened to be impressed; but in one respect, there was perfect unison of feeling. This was that we should fire no blank cartridges at the mob which was giving trouble at home while we were fighting at the front. We had always fought the rebels as a matter of duty but with no personal feeling; but if we could get at a New York mob, we felt certain of being able to teach them a lesson which they would never need to learn again.

Our regiment camped by itself in Washington Square. Soon after [our] going into the square, a citizen came up to me and inquired, "What are you here for?" I told him, "Because we were ordered here." He then asked if we would fire upon the citizens. I replied, "If we are so ordered," and, immediately turning my back, walked away. He afterwards asked Sergeant Pierce about the same questions and received the same answers. He then asked Pierce if we would not use blank cartridges or fire over their heads the first time. Pierce said, "No, we use no blank cartridges and we shoot to kill." The man evidently began to feel, as I did for him, that he had better leave camp.

1. In mid-July, protests against the draft by Irish workingmen in New York City led to four days of savage rioting in which some 120 people were killed. Most of the deaths occurred when police and units of the Army of the Potomac (fresh from Gettysburg) restored order by shooting into the mob (James M. McPherson, *Ordeal by Fire: The Civil War and Reconstruction* [New York, 1982], 360). The Vermont Brigade arrived on the scene in August, when there was no recurrence of the violence.

We took our meals in a large room across Broadway. I marched the men there without arms. The first day, in crossing Broadway, an omnibus attempted to break through the company. One of the men seized the horses by the bit and stopped them. At the same time, I halted the company and passed back to the omnibus. The driver raised his whip to strike the man who held the horses; but just before the blow came down, he glanced towards me and for some reason he did not strike. I at once assured him that if he should so much as let the whip touch the soldier, he would never be able to raise it again. Very deliberately, I started the company and moved it on. We were never again troubled. The New York mobs seemed so perfectly satisfied with the character of our visit that I did not hear of the slightest disturbance while we were in the city. When we reached New York we were just [back] from one of the hardest campaigns of the war. Our faces were bronzed to the color of the dark mulatto. Overcoats and blankets were thrown away, while our clothing was dirty and ragged. The general or expert in military affairs would have looked upon us with pride; the elastic quickstep, reckless and jovial air, with bright rifles, betrayed the veteran soldiery which we were. Citizens doubtless looked upon us with feelings of sympathy, and it was not strange, perhaps, that the little boy visiting our camp should have asked his father if those soldiers had to eat hay.

Our service before this had been among people quite unfriendly, and I could hardly understand what the man wanted when one morning a citizen came in and asked if the men were fond of melons. I told him, "Yes, but the boys have no money." He said, "That does not matter," and in a short time a dray load was driven into the square, and we were told that they were ours. After this we were reminded in many ways that we were among friends and in "God's Country."

In a few days the draft was completed and we were on our way back to our old position in the Army of the Potomac.

After a fall campaign which, so far as we were concerned, consisted in shifting our position, marching, and countermarching, we finally started on the 7th of November for Rappahannock Station.

Our brigade halted in front of the enemy's earthworks, attracting their attention and drawing their fire while General Russell,[2]

2. Brigadier General David Allen Russell.

with the 1st Division of the 6th Corps, was getting between the enemy's works and the river, thus forcing the surrender of nearly 2,000 prisoners. Lieutenant A. F. Coleman, of a rebel Louisiana regiment and my future brother-in-law, was among the prisoners captured.

We immediately crossed the Rappahannock and went into camp just where a rebel regiment had been so recently run out that we found rations cooking over the fire. Their little huts were only partially completed, consequently new and clean, and were immediately utilized by us. We found some muster and clothing rolls here which attracted my attention: first, because the penmanship of the officers who made them was neater and nicer than ours; and second, the enlisted men, almost without exception, made their marks instead of writing their names. We were just nicely fixed for comfort when we were ordered to break camp and start on that expedition south of the Rapidan known as Mine Run.

9

Mine Run, November, 1863

It was the last of November; the ground would freeze at night and thaw during the day, giving us frozen ground to sleep on and mud to march in. After a number of blunders and delays, our corps was marched in the night into the woods in front of the enemy's works with the general understanding that in the morning we were to charge; but wiser councils prevailed, and we returned to our old camp on the Rappahannock.

During this expedition I witnessed the proof of the old saying that "all men are cowards in the dark." The last night of our advance, when from our orders we knew that we were close upon the enemy, the brigade staff a few rods in front halted and faced the marching column. At that instant the moon broke through the clouds and the mounted staff was observed. Someone said, "Masked battery," and instantly every man was out of the road and, if possible, behind a tree; but in a few moments all were in their places again. I think that almost every man with whom I have ever talked about this matter has insisted that he did not get out of the road until he saw everyone else out. The last two days of this expedition our rations were only the toughest of fresh beef, without salt or bread.

The winter of '63 and '64 at Brandy Station, we were very pleasantly situated. We had become such experts at house building that our quarters were comfortable, our rations and clothing abundant and good. The entire corps had white gloves for parade, which, taken in connection with our reputation for good fighting and discipline, gave us many an extra review for the gratification of visitors both native and foreign.

Occasionally, a young officer who had not seen service would be sent on from home with a commission. This was very annoying to the old vets. A common way of welcoming him as he passed along the line would be in the following manner:

"Jim, do you want to make a good trade?"

"Yes."

"Well, buy that fellow for what he is worth and sell him for what he thinks he is worth."

This winter a large number of the Vermont Brigade reenlisted. I was among the number and was sent to Vermont in charge of those of our company who had the veteran furlough.[1] This, it was represented to me, was a favor which should in a measure recompense me for not receiving a promotion to lieutenant, which I considered belonged to me. I was not then crafty enough to understand that my reenlistment was against my getting a commission. By reenlisting, the authorities understood that I intended to stay and fight it out whether I got a commission or not.

After returning from Vermont and discovering that a sergeant had been promoted to lieutenant during my absence, I determined to leave the regiment and at once made application with Sergeant Pierce to be ordered before the examination board at Washington for a commission in the colored troops. This of course met with all possible objection in our command, but we received the order. I passed the examination and was recommended for a captaincy.

1. In the fall and early winter of 1863–1864, veteran soldiers who reenlisted for "three years or the war" received four-hundred-dollar bounties and thirty- to thirty-five-day furloughs. When three-fourths of a company or regiment reenlisted, the men were permitted to go home together.

10

Wilderness Campaign, 1864

The spring of 1864 saw a reorganization of the Army of the Potomac into three corps. Our division [was] strengthened by one brigade, General Getty[1] in command, and U. S. Grant [was] in command of the reorganized army. I felt, and think the feeling was general, that General Meade was a better commander than Grant; but at that time the Army of the Potomac was too much of the veteran to have a simple preference of commanders make any difference with its fighting.

The 3rd of May the army commenced its movement. On the 4th we crossed the Rapidan for the death struggle between two of the grandest armies of veterans which the world has ever seen, and halted for the night just below Germanna Ford. In the morning we moved southward, the road filled with artillery and ammunition trains, while on each side were moving lines of infantry. The march was slow and tedious consequent from the head of the infantry column being compelled to improvise their road through field and wood. Men were heavily loaded [with] rifles, fifty rounds of ammunition, six days' rations, canteen of water, overcoat, blankets, and knapsack filled with clothing. The slow, halting style of moving caused the men to feel keenly the weight of the knapsack, from which they had had ninety days' rest. After about two hours, when the men were in as bad humor as possible, to our surprise and joy we saw General Getty turn to the right into the road. Our regiment that day led the division; consequently, general and staff, with orderly carrying the division flag (a blue flag

1. Brigadier General George Washington Getty, commander of the 2nd Division, VI Corps, Army of the Potomac.

with a white cross, always denoting, on the field and in the camp, division headquarters), was but a few rods in front of us. For half an hour I could hear different regiments cheering as they turned from the field into the road. They were so delighted with the change that for the first two hours they did not notice the rapidity of their march, which was but little short of the double-quick.

The horses of the general and staff kept in a short trot. We began to wonder what this meant. We remembered that as we turned into the road, both Generals Grant and Meade were sitting upon their horses, keenly watching us as we passed by. Meade—tall, straight, neatly dressed in the uniform of the major general— looked every inch the soldier he was; Grant—sitting upon his horse carelessly, cigar in his mouth, coat unbuttoned, hat pulled over his eyes—had more of the appearance of a cavalryman just in from a raid than the General of the Armies.

We remembered that infantry, artillery, and even that monarch of the road, the ammunition wagon, had been pulled aside to give us, a moving column of infantry, a clear road. This was something exceedingly rare. We saw that our division was detached from the corps. From early morn we had been given no rest. Our division— 2nd Division of the 6th Corps, known as the White Cross Division from our badge—was the strongest division in the army. Five of its regiments were from the Green Mountains of Vermont, and the other regiments were perhaps equally as good; and as a whole it partook of many of the qualities of the Swiss of Europe or the Highlanders of Scotland. It had been upon every large field of battle since the commencement of the war [and] had never been repulsed or driven from position. Two years' service had weeded out all men lacking in courage or physically weak, while the division as a whole believed itself invincible. From all of these causes we reasoned that our movement must be important. With the regularity of clockwork, every few minutes the order would come from General Getty, "Keep your men closed up." Officers would repeat the imperative "Close up men" from the head of the column until the sound was lost to me as it was repeated backwards to the rear.

It was customary to give about five minutes' rest after an hour's march, but for three hours this rapid marching and hurrying order continued. Men were complaining, declaring that they could not march farther, scolding and grumbling the whole length of the

line. The imperative "Close up men" was losing its effect; the
regular soldier was about played out; the limit of discipline was
about reached. We were moving rapidly southward, a narrow road
in front, a thick wood on right and left. A longer period than usual
had passed since the head of the column had given us the imperative "Close up men," and we began to hope for a rest. All recognized that we could not continue our movement much longer.
Then from the head of the column the explanation was passed
down from officer to man and from man to man until it was
known by everyone in the division: "Boys, our division has been
selected from the Army of the Potomac to seize and hold the junction of the Brock and Orange Plank roads. The success of the campaign, the safety of the army, is staked upon our succeeding."
Only those who have seen can realize the change. The grumbling
regular at once disappears; the citizen-soldier, fired with patriotism [and] national, state, and corps pride, takes his place. The
strong man who was swearing and grumbling at some weak comrade is at once transformed [in]to the kindest of friends and is
offering to help his comrade by carrying his gun for a while or,
giving that greater proof of friendship, offering a drink of water
from his canteen.

The autocratic martinet officer of a few minutes before is now a
brother to the weaker men in his company, at times carrying their
guns to give them a short rest. The mounted officer watches at
the sides of the road to select some weak man to ride his horse
while he tramps along by his side, the invitation conveyed as if it
would be a favor for the soldier to accept. The general with his
stars, the officer with his bars, and the corporal with his chevrons
are all comrades.

Overcoats and blankets from time to time are thrown aside,
knapsacks dropped, and all without once slacking pace. No
thought or desire for rest, no order or word spoken except an occasional kind word of encouragement or offer of assistance; silently
and swiftly for three hours more the march is continued. The
division of regulars has disappeared, and a division of citizen-
soldiers takes it place, in their hearts a patriotic fire which only
victory can satisfy or death quench, each man breathing a silent
prayer that when the White Cross reached the junction, he might
be there. Suddenly a volley is received by the head of the column,

and the order [is given] "By company into line, load and fire at will" and the battle of the Wilderness commenced.[2]

I will not attempt to describe it. The line of battle extended a distance of about twenty-eight miles and was composed of 100,000 men. It was a desperate struggle at short range, in a thick bush. An hour's fighting and we had gained twenty rods, when the enemy, by reinforcement or some other cause, came upon us in such a heavy column that we were gradually pushed back step by step until we lost nearly four rods; then the men, dropping on their knees the better to shoot under the trees, delivered such a terrific and continuous fire that the enemy halted and finally shrank back. We then remembered the ground we had lost, to us a horrid thought. Captain Lillie, a senior captain, sprang in front of the line and gave the order "Forward." The line moved, the captain fell, and it halted. Lieutenant [Carlos W.] Carr immediately took his place and gave the same order with the same result. As he fell, he turned towards me and said, "You are in command."

I think, and I have been told, that I gave my order at once, but so rapid is the working of the human mind that all of the following thoughts passed through and dictated the order. A glance showed to me that I was the senior officer standing. Upon me fell the responsibility of action, the glory if I succeeded, the disgrace if I failed. I thought of the two years of service, its hardships, sufferings, and horrors, of the laurels won upon fourteen fields of battle, the glories of the White Cross which had floated victoriously over us and which were now four rods in front. I remembered our oft-repeated boast that we never left our wounded in the enemy's hands; and yet, with all our past glories and laurels, they were now lying four rods in front of us. That ground must be retaken by the men who had lost it, or our boasting must be silenced and our claims of superiority forever surrendered. I felt, and knew the men must feel, that to hold our ground was enough to require, and

2. The foregoing passage has the ring of a patriotic speech, probably because that is its origin. In the years that he served as the American consul in Kingston, Twitchell frequently gave public lectures recounting his wartime experiences; his favorite topic was the heroism of Vermont's citizen-soldiers at the Wilderness (Marshall Harvey Twitchell Scrapbook [Microfilm copy in Marshall Harvey Twitchell Papers, Prescott Memorial Library, Louisiana Tech University, Ruston]). The Wilderness and the fight at Spotsylvania Courthouse that immediately followed were the Vermont Brigade's biggest and most costly actions of the war.

my orders were given in a manner to indicate that I would be satisfied with retaking what we had lost; at the same time I appealed to their humanity and pride. I gave the order "Forward till you cover the wounded, and then lie down." Instantaneously, that kneeling line, as if one monster animal by electric current moved, swept over the four rods and threw itself in line, rifle in hand, in front of the farthest wounded man. For a moment I stood proudly exulting over the heroic action of my comrades, endeavoring to keep my eyes from the scattered forms which the movement had cost, when I, like my seniors, fell.

My company of fifty-three men one hour before was left in command of the only sergeant standing, and he had but twenty-one men uninjured. I have heard that a sergeant of Company A carried me to the rear. It seems to me that I passed General Hancock and staff, but I more think it was a kind of dream which came from the desire for General Hancock's arrival, as we knew he and his corps were marching to our relief.

I was told that when [I was] taken back, the surgeon insisted that it was only a waste of time to bother with me; but at the earnest solicitations of Ernest Bellemy, a schoolmate of mine, he finally put a bandage around my head.

The next day about ten a.m., I woke up perfectly conscious and found myself lying upon the ground between two bodies from which life had departed. Men under the direction of Corporal Harris, seemingly not as severely wounded as myself, fixed a shelter to protect me from the sun. Sometime during the day they took off my coat, which was a mass of blood in front, washed it, put it on again, and I was carried into a large tent, where I found Captain Lillie, Amidon, and others of the brigade. My cap was lost and my head swollen so large that I was evidently not a pleasant object to look upon. The pitying looks given me as I was brought in said plainer than words, "Poor fellow, he can't live." Amidon alone had courage enough to say in a lively manner, "We took it pretty rough, didn't we?"

I remember nothing more until the afternoon of the 6th or 7th, when we heard that both armies were moving to the left and that the wounded were to be taken to Fredericksburg, to the extent of the ambulance transportation, and the remainder would be abandoned to the enemy.

Just about dark I asked a hospital attendant when they were

going to take me. He said, "Not at all. The last ambulance has been some time gone. There are no ambulances for dead men." I looked around the tent upon the few silent forms remaining and thought perhaps he was right about them, but he had certainly made a mistake in classing me among their number. I thought of my position for a few moments and made up my mind that I would see if I could stand. After quite a number of failures I succeeded in getting to my feet. My face was so badly swollen that one eye was entirely closed and the other had to be pulled open with my fingers in order to see at all. Keeping my feet well apart and taking short steps, I moved out to the road, found the direction to Fredericksburg, and started. A short distance from the tent I noticed in my front what appeared to be a strip of sand, and the road at that point seemed to be blocked by wounded men waiting for something. I did not know what. I turned, stepped onto the supposed sand, and in a moment was in the Wilderness Brook. I climbed out on the other side completely wet through but found this unexpected bath and thorough wetting of my swollen head a most fortunate occurrence. I marched along a short distance farther and discovered that my weakness would certainly compel a halt. The thought occurred to me that if I fell in the road in the darkness, I would surely be trod upon until life was extinct, and so, noticing two little trees on one side, I dropped down between them, thinking that they would protect me in this respect. My next remembrance is of the morning, when I heard a man say, "I think he belongs to the Vermont Brigade on account of the White Cross which he has upon his breast. You had better put him into the ambulance."

I have since learned that it was a detachment of the 1st Vermont Cavalry which was passing that picked me up. Lieutenant Stone of the 1st Vermont had charge of the ambulances, which doubtless explains the reason for my remaining in them as they followed the cavalry on its raid to the rear of Lee's army. I heard Stone say that he was ordered to have the ambulances all clear and that there was no place to leave me except on the ground in the open field. I expected this would be my fate, but I presume he forgot to remove me.

I remember nothing as to time or place, with the exception that the horses seemed to be upon a sharp trot all of the time and that a man of the 1st Vermont, wounded in the foot, was put into the ambulance with me. I think it was the last night passed in the ambulance that my wound commenced bleeding, and after endeavoring in vain to waken someone, I lay down with the thought that it would bleed less if I kept quiet and that my career, civil and military, was ended. My first consciousness after this was of someone putting a new bandage on my head. I learned that the driver, sleeping under the ambulance, had been wakened by the blood dropping in his face. I can recall but little of what passed the next day until I was taken out and carried into a church at Fredericksburg. The seats had been moved from the building, and we were placed in rows as close together as we could lie on the floor.

After a few hours a hospital attendant came in with a black cup full of beef tea (water in which beef had been boiled) and called my name. I held up my hand. He came along and lifted up my head, saying, "Here, d—— you, by order of," someone I could not understand the name, "drink this." I drank part of it and asked him to give some to the man on my right. His reply was, "Drink, or I will pour it down you." This was all the attention that I saw anyone get in the church. I do not remember whether it was that night or the next day that a surgeon called out, "All who can ride in a baggage wagon can have a chance to go to Aquia Creek." By lack of exertion I had been left once; therefore, I immediately commenced making efforts to get to my feet. A man lying near me, wounded in the leg but with a good stock of strength in his arms, assisted me to rise. Someone helped me along to the side of the church, and with my hand against the wall, I successfully made the trip around the door. An assistant surgeon, glancing at my uniform, said, "I have orders to take none but cavalry." I immediately stepped back out of the line, took off my coat, and in a few moments again came before him to be helped into the wagon. He asked me if I belonged to the cavalry. My ambulance companion, who had just got in, answered, "Yes, he belongs to my company." My place was right over the hind axle, and as we started away from the church door to make room for another wagon, I felt certain that I would not be able to stand the jar over the corduroy road[3] to Aquia Creek.

Looking out, I saw a negro woman shyly putting her head out of

---

3. A road surface of thick branches and small tree trunks laid perpendicular to the route.

the cabin window. I motioned for her to come to me and asked if she could get me a bundle of straw to sit on. She said, "No massa, but I can give you my pillow." I took the pillow and gave her what small change I had. It was nearly dark before the train moved out on the road for the Potomac. The only incident which occurred during the night was being halted by guerrillas, who quickly detached two fine horses from an ambulance containing General Torbert[4] and got away with them.

At Aquia Creek we met some members of the Christian Commission,[5] who gave me a fine cup of coffee of which I was greatly in need. My condition at this time was certainly very bad. I had not been able to take any food since I was wounded, could open my mouth only just far enough to insert a spoon, and I had lived up to that time on a little beef broth which had been given me, to the best of my recollection, only twice. As I staggered along to the boat, the guard let down his gun, saying that the boat was loaded. A member of the Christian Commission, who I afterwards learned was a son of Governor Holbrook,[6] was passing off the boat just at that time. He raised the bayonet, holding it for me to pass on as he went off, the boat moving from the bank at the same time.

I fell asleep as soon as I was on the transport and have no remembrance of the trip up the Potomac or of being placed in the hospital. From the time I was wounded I was in constant fear of losing my mind on account of the wounds being in my head. I opened my eyes in the hospital, found that I was undressed and in a narrow bed upon which, to my surprise, were white sheets. The room was very large and filled with beds, all of which were occupied. Then, as I looked to the centre of the room, I saw a lady sitting at a desk. I closed my eyes in despair and tried to think of all I had recently experienced—the battlefield and its horrors, wounded comrades, no attention, my journey on the boat, and now a clean bed with sheets like home and a woman. It must be that what I have feared has at last come to pass and I am crazy. As I opened my eyes again, the lady noticed me and came to the bed and asked me how I felt. I replied, "Quite well, thank you." She smiled and returned to her desk. Hours passed away before I fully

4. Brigadier General Alfred Thomas Torbert, commander of the 1st Cavalry Division, Army of the Potomac.
5. The voluntary relief organization of the Young Men's Christian Association.
6. Frederick Holbrook, Republican governor of Vermont, 1861–1863.

realized that I was in one of Uncle Sam's hospitals in my right mind, and the lady was the nurse in charge—one of those grand representatives of her sex who had left the ease and luxuries of her Northern home to nurse back to life and strength the wounded defenders of her country.

I had seen so much suffering and death that the placing of a screen around the cot of a dying comrade did not materially affect me, but the number of wounds washed with the same sponge and from the same basin made me feel that my recovery would be more certain if I was at home. My money and clothes had been taken from me, so I had nothing to do but lie in bed and think.

I soon decided upon a plan to get out of the hospital. When the surgeon came I asked him to make me out a furlough, telling him that there was no need of my being cared for by the government, that my people could do it just as well at home. I called on the matron for my money very often and purchased fruit and other things which the authorities would allow us to have, being very free with my eatables and also with my money, never taking back any small change. This and my large talk to the attendants convinced them that I was something more than an ordinary orderly sergeant. I soon succeeded in getting the surgeon to promise me a furlough. After he had left the office I sent for the hospital steward and persuaded him to have it made out. The next morning I secured the surgeon's signature, but he told the hospital steward that it was only done to keep me quiet, that he must not give me the leave yet. This I learned from the clerk. The next morning, as the surgeon was leaving the ward, I called to him and asked him if I could have some oranges. Of course he said, "Yes." As he was passing by the steward's room, I called him again and asked him what he said. He answered back, "Yes," and left the ward.

After I became certain that he was safely away, I asked the matron for my clothing. She replied that she had not been notified to give them to me. The steward said that I had no leave, finally admitted that it was made out but that the surgeon did not order him to let me have it. I then asked him if he did not hear the surgeon say "Yes" as he was going past his door. They all wanted to accommodate me, and the evidence was so strong in my favor that they concluded I was right and gave me my clothes. I soon had them on with my leave of absence in my hand and was in the ambulance for the depot. Here to my surprise I met the surgeon, who was seeing his wounded men on board the train. He stopped me, saying I had no leave, was not fit, and should not go. I told him I had my leave, and if I was not able to go, he should not have signed it and that we should have a row before I gave up the furlough. I presume he thought the easiest way out of the difficulty was the best; consequently, he let me pass. We entered the car and soon started homeward. I rode standing as long as I possibly could for fear that the jar of the running train would again open my wound.

After we reached Philadelphia it seemed as though the people could not do enough for us. It was one continual ovation from there to Vermont. Just as I was passing out of Brattleboro I heard a rooster crow. I involuntarily turned to see who was going to jump out and catch him.

My mother, as I raced home, had just received my letter dictated from the hospital. A few hours afterwards she learned from a letter written by a comrade on the battlefield that I was among the killed. My reception seemed to me very strange. I felt pleased to be safely at home once more and with my rough army experience could hardly understand why they should all be so sad.

For one hundred days I remained at home, petted by everyone; and notwithstanding my confinement in a darkened room for two or three weeks on account of my eyes, and the occasional removal of a piece of bone from my face, the time passed pleasantly and rapidly.

In August I visited Saratoga Springs and returned by stage over the mountains through the district in Winhall where I had taught school. I boarded with Mr. Johnson most of the time while there. [When] I [first] called at his shop, he looked up, dropped iron and hammer, and with a pale face exclaimed, "My God, ain't you dead?" He had not heard the corrected report and supposed that I was killed at the Wilderness. On reaching home I found a notification from the hospital that I had been appointed captain, and immediately started for Washington.

11

In the 109th Regiment, U.S. Colored Troops, 1864–1865

There [in Washington] I received transportation and orders for Louisville, Kentucky. At Louisville, with a number of other unassigned officers, I was used for organizing colored troops.

I was informed by the adjutant that being only a convalescent I would be allowed to pass the guard, go to the city when I pleased, and drill my company when I pleased. I occasionally availed myself of the opportunity of a visit into town but never failed to drill my company its full time. My experience as drillmaster in the 4th Vermont enabled me to work my men up to such a position that I received a direct compliment from Colonel Hammond[1] at the Sunday morning inspection. Monday morning, much to my disgust, I was directed to turn my company over to a lieutenant and form a new one for myself, retaining at the same time an oversight over the old one.

I obeyed orders and sullenly went to work forming a new company. After drill I made written application to be sent to my regiment, waited a few days, and called on Colonel Hammond. He said it had been forwarded to General Chetlain,[2] commanding the Louisville district.

I went down to the city, called at General Chetlain's office, and there learned that my application had been disapproved because Colonel Hammond had said that he could not spare me. Fortunately for me, General Thomas,[3] Adjutant General of the Army, was in Louisville on a tour of inspection. His office was on a boat

1. Lieutenant Colonel John H. Hammond, commander of the Louisville conscript depot.
2. Brigadier General Augustus Louis Chetlain.
3. Brigadier General Lorenzo Thomas, who was also the officer in charge of recruiting black troops for the entire Mississippi Valley.

then at the wharf. I turned my steps to the river. Arriving there an aide informed me that the general was lying down in his stateroom. Saying I would wait, I took a seat. I presume the aide concluded from the expression on my face that I had come to stay, for in a few minutes he opened the stateroom door and motioned for me to enter. The general looked up, pointed to the scar on my face, and asked where I received it. I said, "In the Wilderness battle." "What do you want of me?" was his next inquiry. I told him that I wished to be ordered to my regiment. Calling to the aide, he said, "Give the boy what he wants, I like to accommodate such lads," pointing again to the scar.

In a few hours I was on my way to Louisa, Kentucky, where the 109th Colored Infantry, to which I had been assigned, was stationed. I reported to Colonel [Orion A.] Bartholomew, then in command, early in September and was assigned to the command of Company H. Since its organization this company had been drilled by different officers, each one doubtless feeling that his command was only temporary; consequently, the discipline had fallen so low that it was rightfully considered the fag end of the regiment. On account of my youthful looks some of the officers prophesied to the colonel that Company H would get away with their boy captain.

It took the first two days to get acquainted with my men and their faults. The third day, after having previously given emphatic notice of changes that must be made, I commenced taking the names of delinquents and at dark had them report to my tent with arms, knapsacks, and accoutrements, ready for a long march. I drilled the squad until nine p.m. After that I rarely had but one delinquent at a time, so I used to put him on a beat in heavy marching order in front of my tent. In a very short time the character of Company H was entirely changed, and my punishments occurring after dark were but little known outside of the company.

It was while stationed here that I received the unexpected notice of the death of my father, whom I had left in good health in Vermont only a few weeks before.

In October we received orders to join the eastern army and, on the 24th, camped just outside of Baltimore, where I was mustered in. One night there was an alarm given by the guard, and the colonel found that he, the adjutant, and myself were the only officers in camp. There were so many absent without leave that he could not put them under arrest. Here I had my first picture taken in the uniform of a captain and had a good deal of trouble to get my mustache black enough to show. The task required could only be accomplished by a liberal use of hair dye.

From Baltimore we went up the James River, halting finally near Fort Harrison, our regiment forming part of the front line, within a few miles of Richmond, in Shaw's[4] brigade, Birney's[5] division of the 25th Army Corps, Army of the James. Here I was again, after seven months' absence, in a large army investing Richmond. Twenty feet in front of our camp was a fine breastwork strengthened by ditch and abatis. A half mile beyond, in plain view, were the enemy's pickets, while at our right and left, far beyond the reach of our vision, extended our line of camp. This seemed natural and homelike to me but quite new to my men.

One day, while grading our streets, we unearthed the body of one of the many "unknown" who fell in the struggle. My only course was to dig a deep grave by his side, place him in it, and leave him buried in our company street.

The splendid and perfect soldiers which these men were making, excelling even the best white troops I had ever seen, caused me to look forward with intense interest to their first battle. By the time we had reached this advance camp, changes had taken place in the regiment until I was the ranking captain. The road to the front from the landing on the James River was almost impassable on account of the mud. Our regiment was detailed for one day's work building corduroy roads. I was in command, and as I halted at corps headquarters to report, I found, to my pleasant surprise, as A[ssistant] A[djutant] G[eneral] my former schoolmate and comrade of the 4th Vermont, Dan D. Wheeler. My colored regiment was much better at fatigue duty than white men, although they had become soldierly enough to be quite noisy and required the close attention of the officers to prevent them from shirking.

Sometime during the day a staff officer from General Butler's[6] headquarters came with an order for me to keep my men quiet,

4. Colonel James Shaw, Jr.
5. Brigadier General William Birney was the older brother of General David Bell Birney and the son of the famous Southern-born abolitionist James Gillespie Birney.
6. Major General Benjamin F. Butler, commander of the Army of the James. Butler was relieved of command January 7, 1865; this was possibly the "disagreeable news from Washington" referred to in this paragraph.

saying that the general would put the entire regiment, officers and men, in the guardhouse if it were not done. At my expression of surprise that a major general should make a threat so unmilitary, he said that "the old general had just received some disagreeable news from Washington and did not care for military law." I immediately sent an order along the line to commanders of companies to send all noisy men back into the woods to a fire. In this way General Butler's command was obeyed, but at the expense of almost stopping the work.

One day the enemy commenced a vigorous shelling of our camp. Immediately my company moved behind the works. Some of the other officers followed my example. While waiting for orders, Adjutant Smith informed me that I was in command of the regiment, that the 119th on our left was out, and the 109th was all there was left to defend both fronts and the fort. I immediately sent Captain [Edward D.] Keplinger with two companies to the fort, spreading the other eight behind the works. Just as my arrangements were completed and I had mounted the fortifications to see if the enemy was preparing to charge, General Birney and staff came up and inquired how I had disposed my men. I informed him and he approved of my action. We learned afterwards that this shelling was only to call our attention from an intended attack south of the James.

Captain Keplinger was wounded during the shelling. The troops behaved splendidly. This attack brought me before the notice of General Birney, so that I was detailed to command a picked company of skirmishers. Colonel Bartholomew made representations at headquarters that he had but one field officer and he needed me for major; consequently, the detail was cancelled. From this time on I did no detail duty except as a field officer. The last picket duty done by me was as brigade field officer of the day. Brigadier General [Richard Henry] Jackson, a very large man, was corps field officer. He made a visit to the outside pickets and asked me whether we had better ride from right to left, or from left to right. There had been a good deal of firing, and I thought that two mounted officers with showy sashes over their shoulders would certainly draw the enemy's fire and immediately told him that I thought it was better to go from right to left. That, I knew, would bring him between me and the enemy. I looked upon it as foolishness in him to take the ride, but he knew better than I did that an agreement had just been made to stop picket firing. I do not presume he ever knew why I thought that from the right to the left was the proper course.

The last of March, just before the commencement of the Appomattox campaign, our division was reviewed by President Lincoln. The last time I ever saw the martyred President was as I saluted in passing by in front of my well-drilled regiment.

Before the month was out we had crossed the south bank of the James and were in front of Petersburg. On the day we were taking position for the general charge and while the regiment was under sharp artillery fire, I took the responsibility of changing the course of the regiment from moving to the left in four ranks, to moving to the front in line of battle. The colonel was at the head of the regiment and could not see that we were uncovered, and the bursting shells doubtless prevented his hearing the order. I presume he thought it was Colonel Shaw's order, or [because of his] seeing and recognizing that it was the proper thing to do, I heard nothing from it, as I feared that I might. That night a brigade detail was made to go out front and throw out a redoubt behind which we could place a battery for the support of the charge in the morning. Colonel [James T.] Bates was in command of the detail, and without making inquiry in reference to ranking captain, placed me in command, and himself went back to brigade headquarters. The men were working very quietly and industriously when they were stampeded by a volley from the enemy. [They] dropped their shovels, ran over me, and for half a minute things looked discouraging; but almost without exception they obeyed my orders and came back to the works. I learned that when the volley was heard at brigade headquarters, Bates was asked whom he left in command. He replied, "Captain Twitchell." Someone else immediately said, "Well, we shall hear more then, before he is driven in." They had more confidence in me at that time, I am afraid, than I had in myself.

Colonel Bartholomew and myself crept close out to the enemy's pickets during the night to learn the lay of the land and discover the obstacles which we would have to encounter the next day. In forming for the charge the following morning, the 109th was in mass, double column on the centre, officers not ordered in rear of the division. This placed me two paces in front of the column, but a few feet from the colors. In fact, I could see that, whether intentionally or not, I was placed where my movements would guide the regiment. For a minute or two, while waiting for the order, I passed along in front of our division, told them that the old 6th Corps, the best in the army and the one in which I had served, would charge on our right and that they would now have an opportunity of proving whether they were men or only fit for slaves. The order came and we swept across the field. The alignment of the regiment was perfect. As I reached the abatis I looked back; the men were so wild and determined that I felt nothing would stop them. Neither abatis nor ditch did stop them; tearing the one away, jumping and tumbling over the other, there was not a halt until the inside of the works was reached and the order received.

Lee's line was broken and there was nothing for us but rapid marching in pursuit until we reached Appomattox Courthouse. The morning of the surrender we were again formed in line to charge. Just before the order, the white flag was raised and the war was over.

12

Texas Expedition, 1865

In a few hours we were on the march for City Point, where we were to embark for the Southwest, our brigade being one of those that was to be used in the formation of a new army to look after Confederate and Maximilian[1] combinations. I think it was during the second day's march that we were horrified by the news of Lincoln's assassination. While we were stopping at City Point, my company presented me with a sword, Lieutenant C[harles] W. Smith making the presentation speech.

The propeller *Clyde* took us from Fortress Monroe to Fort St. Philip on the Mississippi River. Here we disembarked, the propeller going up to New Orleans for supplies. The moat around Fort St. Philip was filled with alligators, and the mosquitoes, from their enormous size, were nearly as dangerous and much more troublesome.

One night a young alligator crept out of the moat, crawled up into one of the tents, and put his cold nose upon a man's face. He opened his eyes and with an unearthly yell jumped into the air, taking the little tent with him. The frightened alligator slid back into the stream. We tried to make the man believe that it was not an alligator but a mosquito that had disturbed his slumbers.

From Fort St. Philip we took transport for Indianola, Texas. The wharf had been burned, and it was a good half mile from where

1. Archduke Ferdinand Maximilian of Austria was made Emperor of Mexico in 1864 by the intervention of Napoleon III. Immediately after the Civil War, the United States demanded French withdrawal and moved fifty thousand soldiers to the Rio Grande under Major General Philip H. Sheridan. Heeding the warning, Napoleon III pulled his troops out in 1867, and the Mexicans executed the hapless Maximilian.

the *Clyde* was anchored to the beach in front of the town. An examination with field glasses presented to all appearances a deserted town. But it was not thought best to trust appearances. Colonel Bartholomew directed me to take two companies and make an investigation. We had boats for only one; therefore, I took my own and was myself the first man to land. [I] put the company in line and sent the boats back for the other. Deploying the first company as skirmishers, using the second as reserve, we entered the town of Indianola and placed our flag upon the courthouse. The next day we crossed a little arm of the bay to a peninsula to select a campground for the regiment. The water was very poor and could not be used without boiling. I managed to get on good terms with the occupants of the only house there and was supplied with good drinking water from their cistern, a favoritism not much liked by the other officers.

One afternoon a detail of half a dozen officers was ordered to report at brigade headquarters at dark. We learned that there was a troublesome desperado back in the country whom we were to make an attempt to kill or capture. We mounted mustangs provided for the purpose and with our native guide started about nine p.m. It seemed to me that it was a steady lope all night. Just before day we surrounded the house, but the bird had flown. We were surprised to find that our mustangs were apparently fresher after their all night's ride than we were.

Soon after this a board of survey was called to inspect some commissary stores. First Lieutenants [Julius H.] Higley, [John M.] Schoonmaker, and [Charles E.] Hart, with some other officers whom I do not remember, were on the board. As we were returning to camp, the boat swamped and we were thrown into the water; the wind was high, and the tide running strong seaward. I swam a few minutes, looked back, and saw that the others were not gaining in the least and that if anyone reached the camp and gave the alarm, it must be me. I reached the shore but so completely exhausted that I could only give the alarm and have a boat sent out after my comrades. The first thing that the droll Higley said upon stepping out of the boat was that he thought when in the water that there would be a fine time that night in camp among the second lieutenants at the good prospect for their promotion.

It had just become settled that there was to be no more fighting when, for the first time in my life, I had a severe toothache. The brigade surgeon informed me that he had no instruments, but said, "This is a fine chance for you to go to New Orleans. I can order you up there for medical treatment." I willingly accepted the offer and was soon in the city, put up at the City Hotel, and that night went to the theatre. While there my old schoolmate Captain L[emuel] I. Winslow saw me, and for the next three days we had a pleasant time looking about New Orleans.

When I returned to Indianola, it was to turn over my company and [go] back [to New Orleans] on detached service in the Freedmen's Bureau under the command of Assistant Commissioner Conway.[2] I found the officers of the 109th far from being pleased at my leaving the regiment. There were none too many, they thought, for social enjoyment when all were present. The day I was to leave, the bay was so rough that no small boat could pass between the steamer and the shore. The next day it was a little smoother, and a boat from a Mexican schooner came in. I went down to the beach [and] found the captain of an American ship negotiating with the Mexican to take him out to his ship. I at once had myself included in the contract. I felt that the chances were very much against my reaching the steamer on account of the high sea, and should not have ventured alone. As the captain left me for his vessel, he said in English, "Don't let them d—— Mexicans make any excuse for stopping at their sloop. They would cut your throat and throw you overboard for your clothes. If they don't head for the steamer, you point to her with one hand and your revolver at them with the other. They will readily obey, for they are great cowards." The captain misjudged the Mexicans; I was soon on board the steamer. Upon arriving at New Orleans, I took quarters with my friend Winslow in one of the fine abandoned houses of the Garden District.

2. Thomas W. Conway was head of the Freedmen's Bureau in Louisiana. Twitchell wrongly identifies him as a brigadier general; he was a civilian and his correct title has been substituted.

13

Provost Marshal and
Freedmen's Bureau Agent,
1865–1866

After a few days, in full uniform I reported to Commissioner Conway. The careless dress and unmilitary manners at his headquarters gave me my first lesson of the semi-civil duties of my new assignment. It was here that I was introduced to Edward W. Dewees, a boyish-looking fellow in civilian dress and, it seemed to me, much too young for a chief of detective police.[1] I little thought of the dangerous and exciting future which would bind us together like brothers.

I was informed at headquarters that I was to be appointed provost marshal and agent of the Freedmen's Bureau for the parish of Bienville or Claiborne, that I might have my choice. I selected Bienville and received my orders, dated October 24, 1865. I drew a fine black Morgan horse from the quartermaster department and, with an order on General A. J. Smith[2] for troops, started up the river for Sparta, the parish seat of Bienville. The boat was a little

1. Dewees was a special officer of the Louisiana Provost Marshal General of Freedmen and is described in official correspondence as the "chief of the Detective Force Bureau of Freedmen" (Letters Received by the Louisiana Assistant Commissioner, 1865, Bureau of Refugees, Freedmen, and Abandoned Lands, Record Group 105, National Archives, 79, 301, 322, 325). Most likely he was from New York (United States Civil Service Commission, *Official Register of the United States,* 1867). Although Twitchell spells his name *Deweese* throughout the autobiography, almost all other documents, including those signed by Dewees himself, have it *Dewees.* Here, and in subsequent pages, Dewees' full first name *Edward* has been substituted for the initial *E.* I have followed this practice with respect to members of Twitchell's family and his close associates.
2. Major General Andrew J. Smith, commander of the western district of Louisiana in Alexandria.

stern-wheel, so loaded with passengers that nearly all the men had to sleep on the floor. I was the only one in uniform and consequently came in for a good share of notice. The first annoying speech which I overheard was at Alexandria. As I passed by some workmen, one spoke, motioning his head towards me, and said to a comrade, "There goes one of our bosses."

General Smith endorsed my order for the troops and sent me on to Shreveport. At this place I made the acquaintance of Brevet Brigadier General [William S.] Mudgett, Lieutenant Colonel [Charles W.] Keeting, Lieutenants [J. H.] McVean and [James L.] Thompson—Mudgett commanding the post, Keeting provost marshal of the city, [and] Thompson quartermaster.

I went out into the country twice to assist in making contracts between freedmen and their employers. Once [I visited] upon the plantation of Mr. Howell, whose brother was afterwards killed at Coushatta. After this last journey I came to the conclusion that the story which the officers had been telling me, "that it was not safe to go through to Minden without a guard," was partly to keep me there for the purpose of making their own duty lighter. So one morning I ordered my horse and with a single orderly set out through the swamp for Minden, which I reached before dark. I learned there that a few days before, Captain Graff[3] had been sent down from Minden with a detachment to Sparta; consequently, I would have nothing to do but to go on the next morning and relieve Captain Graff.

I reached Sparta the next afternoon without incident and the next morning received the command, stores, and supplies from Captain Graff, and he at once returned to Minden. I now found myself twenty-five miles from the nearest military post in command of a detachment of United States Colored Infantry, about twenty men with horses for only about fifteen.

I was surrounded by a community in which there were at least one thousand disbanded Confederate soldiers, all having no love for the government which had just vanquished them and of which I was the representative. There was an intense bitterness against the colored soldiers, once their slaves but now, under my direction, their masters. In case of needing assistance, I was without

3. Captain Charles S. Graff was the commander of I Company, 61st Regiment, United States Colored Troops, in Minden.

telegraph, railway, or water connection. The government of the people was entirely with me, with no authority from which to receive instructions nearer than New Orleans, to which place a paper could not go at that time in less than five days. I am free to confess that had I known beforehand what my position was to be, I should have remained with my regiment.

I selected for my office the room in the courthouse which had formerly been used as the jury room. My men quartered in a vacant house about ten rods from there. My first work I thought should be to attend to the occupants of the jail. I found no charges against anyone among the captain's papers and asked the sergeant what that girl whom I had seen there was in jail for. He said he did not know, so I ordered her before me and inquired the reason. She could not tell but said that Mrs. Pearce was mad at her anyway, and she presumed that was the cause for her being arrested.

Mrs. Pearce was the wife of Lieutenant Governor Pearce,[4] the most prominent [man] in town. The governor was absent, and this girl, reported to be his illegitimate daughter, usually received marks of Mrs. Pearce's disapproval of her existence whenever the governor was gone. I walked over to Mrs. Pearce's and as she declined to make any complaint against the girl, I immediately released her, thereby emptying the jail.

I then commenced a study of my instructions concerning the parish and people around me. My duty was to inform both black and white of their changed relations from master and slave to employer and employee, giving them the additional information that it was the order of the government that old master and old slave should remain where they had been [and] work as usual in the harvesting of the crop, at which time I would fix the pay of the ex-slave in case he and his former master did not agree about the amount. I expected all to obey and should not hesitate to enforce obedience from both employer and employee. Corporal punishment must not be restored by the planters, but all cases requiring extreme measures must be reported to me for settlement.

I now came to the question as to how this should be made known to the people scattered over the entire country, two-thirds of them unable to read and no paper published through which I

4. Benjamin W. Pearce was lieutenant governor of Confederate Louisiana, 1864–1865.

could reach the others. While [I was] pondering over this question, the sergeant came in and informed me that a great many men were coming into town from the country and he feared that something was going to happen. Directing my company to stay at their quarters, I hailed the first man I met with the question of what was the occasion of so many being in town? He informed me that the Masonic lodge met there that day. I at once made myself known as a member of that order and secured the services of the Masons—who, then as now, included all the leading elements of society in Bienville Parish—to give notice to all the people that I would be at five different villages in the parish the next week and would there give both black and white their instructions. The notice was faithfully distributed. The gatherings at each place were so great that no attempt was made to get them into any public building, but I spoke to them from the veranda of some house.

The first dispute sufficiently grave to require any investigation was the case of a white man who had struck his old foreman with a stick. I immediately sent a mounted orderly to his plantation with an order for him, the black man, and two colored witnesses to report at my office the next morning; and as the distance was considerable, he [the planter] was directed to furnish the three black men with mules.

The first man I saw in the morning was the plaintiff. In answer to my question of why he walked to town, he said the old master was mad and he was afraid to ask him for a mule. In due time the others arrived and I commenced the proceedings. I found a large audience of spectators curious to see how I was going to manage a case in which all the different powers of legislature and court were combined in one person, who was also the judge.

I ordered the sergeant to take the defendant and witnesses out of the room, then called upon the plaintiff to state his case. After this the defendant was called in for the same purpose, then the first witness. To my relief I found that they all agreed so well that I was having no difficulty in arriving at the facts.

In substance, the planter had three times repeated an order to his foreman in regard to a fence to keep the hogs from the corn. The last time, upon finding the hogs in the field, he had struck him with a stick, but without inflicting any personal injury.

As he was there I thought I would call in the other witness. To my great surprise he made out a case of such bad treatment that I think the plaintiff must have wondered that he was alive. I could see in the audience that there was the most intense interest as to what my decision would be; even the negroes showed much curiosity about the matter. The planters felt that their crops could not be gathered if their hands could obey or not as they might choose.

I told the plaintiff that the defendant had no right to strike him but that he had done him no injury, which was more than I could say of the corn crop which had suffered by his disobedience of orders, and that I would warn him not to again disobey a proper order, and the defendant not to again use a stick; and [I] dismissed the case so far as they were concerned. I then turned to my lying witness and told him that as a slight punishment for the lies he had told me he could walk home and allow the plaintiff to ride his mule. This decision seemed to the people as unique as it was just and gave to all a feeling of relief and confidence. My treatment of the lying negro had so much in it of the comical that it became a standard threat when one was telling a large story for someone to say, "Look out now or you will have to walk home."

For the next three months I was engaged in settling disputes, generally trivial, between the people and explaining to ex-master and slave their respective rights under the new order of things. My disapprobation of lying, as shown in my first case, had in my opinion great effect in lightening my work. It was very rare that I found occasion to go outside of the interested parties to arrive at the facts. In dealing with cases, riding over the parish, and coming in contact with all the different classes of people, it was an exceptional day that I did not find something new or have some of my preconceived ideas swept away. I found the mulattoes did not owe their existence to the white men nearest the social equal of the colored but, on the contrary, to the very highest in social and official life. So far as the forms of religion were concerned, there seemed to be a good percentage of the people Christians.

As I came into dinner one day, I heard my landlady talking in language not very choice to one of the negro girls. We were all seated at the table, and I was wondering how, in her high temper, she was going to ask a blessing, as was her usual custom, when she suddenly dropped her head and said, "Lord bless our food if I be mad," and then continued her scolding.

Another day I rode into the country to a planter's house to divide the cotton. While [they were] weighing it, through the carelessness of one of the negroes, the end of the stick fell upon the old master's head. I never heard a more profane and violent cursing than he gave to the man, and I in my simplicity thought that my presence alone saved the negro from assault. The work however was soon done, and the dinner was announced. It was more than a surprise to me when the planter bowed his head and asked a long and fervent blessing which would have done credit to a doctor of divinity.

At another time, when seated at the table, a minister of the gospel stated with apparent feeling as he grasped his knife, "I would like to cut the heart out of them," referring to some people who differed from him politically.

I found the different religious denominations to be Methodist, Baptist, a few Presbyterians, and one which was new to me termed Hardshell Baptist. This last had for one of its religious ordinances the washing of each other's feet. Three miles from Sparta they had a church. One Sabbath morning, dressed in my new uniform and in company with a young man of the village, we started for the Hardshell Baptist meeting.

The church was a log structure without windows or floor, [with] wooden benches for seats and a pulpit of such height that the minister's feet were on a level with the heads of his listeners when they were standing up. We found the building filled and service had commenced. No person noticed us as we entered, each one being expected to find his own seat, which under the guidance of my friend we soon accomplished. The people were devout and attentive, men seated on one side of the house and women on the other, all dressed in the homespun suits of the country, women wearing homespun sunbonnets absolutely devoid of all attempt at ornament, simplifying, if not entirely doing away with, the feminine church duty of examining their neighbors' bonnets. When I dressed for church it did not occur to me that a bright new uniform with its brass buttons and shoulder straps was not the proper thing to wear. In a few moments I discovered the minister was reproving me for appearing in the house of God in the gaudy dress of war. But in time he dropped me and, I suppose, returned to the discourse which I had interrupted. He next surprised me by saying "that when Jesus Christ, that *fellow*, was on earth, etc." No one else in the audience seemed to look upon the remark as irreverent or anything strange. As I was beginning to think his sermon a very long one, he suddenly stopped speaking and looked fixedly at some object up at the ridgepole of the building. I glanced upward, too, but could see nothing unusual. I looked around over the audience; their heads were all bowed, while I seemed to be the only uneasy person in the building. I at once settled back in my seat to await further developments. After a long and painful silence, the minister said, as he descended from the pulpit, "I have lost my thread." Another man took his place, talked a few minutes, and closed the meeting. I rode home thinking the Hardshell Baptists were a strange people.

Afterwards I learned to respect them for their honesty, industry, and general law-abiding character. Almost entirely nonslaveholders, they were much more free from the vices of the institution than either the slave-holders or that class of whites who lived under their especial patronage.

One day, upon returning from a visit in the country, I found the town in the highest state of excitement. The soldiers were in their quarters with rifles in hand, while many of the citizens were also armed and all parties anxiously waiting for my arrival. I made a rapid investigation and discovered that the cause of the difficulty was in itself so small that it was almost impossible to discover exactly what it was. The people complained only of one man by the name of Harris.[5] The soldiers admitted that insulting language had been used by him, but said that the citizens had threatened to attack all of them. I ordered Harris to remain in his quarters until I had made an examination of the citizens as to what had caused the insulting and threatening language from both parties.

The next morning the sergeant reported to me that Harris had packed his knapsack and said he was going to Shreveport. I had decided in my mind that to send him back to his regiment would be the best thing to do, on account of the ill feeling between him and some of the people, which seemed to be altogether personal. I could not permit the citizens to use threatening language to the soldiers, although they claimed that no threats were made, only against Harris for his insulting language. But Harris could not be

5. Private Wallace Harris and the other soldiers in the detachment were from F Company, 80th Regiment, United States Colored Troops, headquartered in Shreveport.

allowed to walk off to Shreveport without my order, and I did not believe that he would seriously make the attempt.

Shortly after the sergeant left my room, Mr. Love,[6] a citizen, stepped to my door and informed me that Harris, with his rifle, had left and was going towards Shreveport. I immediately ran out and told him to halt and ordered him back to his quarters. He brought his rifle to the ready, but before he could bring it to his shoulder, he fell from a shot coming from behind me. Love had followed me out, and when Harris brought his rifle to the ready, had fired, as he swore, to save my life, saying that I had no idea of the desperate character of Harris. Love was arrested and taken to Shreveport, examined, and released.[7] I have no doubt but that Love believed that Harris was going to shoot me, but I have always been in doubt whether he [Harris] was preparing to shoot me or whether he had seen Love and was getting ready for him.

The arrest of Love, in connection with bad whisky, had the effect of giving me a little annoyance the next afternoon. A drunken desperado met me on the street and commenced complaining about the presence of negro soldiers, flourishing his revolver until he had exhausted my patience.[8] I told him to put it up and come over to the grocery with me. When I said to the barkeeper, "Here is a customer of yours whom you will certainly lose if he annoys me any more today," I think the deliberate coolness with which I informed them that after that notice I should kill him made even his drunken brain perceive that his provocations must cease.

During my boyhood I had heard and read of the palatial residences with splendid furnishings and luxurious living of the Southern planter, and as I had thus far seen dwellings hardly comfortable, without a carpet on the floor, [the inhabitants] living

6. Robert B. Love, a Sparta grocer.

7. The fatal shooting occurred on December 18, 1865. Love and Private Harris had had an altercation in the street the day before. Lieutenant Colonel Orrin McFadden of the 80th Regiment, United States Colored Troops, investigated the incident and concluded that it was *"Premeditated Murder."* He was probably right, but the time and place made it difficult to hold Love accountable, not only because Harris was black but also because the region was characterized by rough, frontier-style justice. Harris had a rifle in his hands, and there was just enough plausibility in Love's claim to be defending Twitchell to create reasonable doubt. McFadden's report is in Harris' Compiled Military Service Record, Record Group 94, National Archives.

8. The beginning of this paragraph is confusing because the connection, if any, between the "arrest of Love" and the "drunken desperado" is not made clear.

generally on corn and bacon, I was beginning to entirely disbelieve these early stories. I received a call one day from the son of one of the wealthiest planters, with the request from his father that I come out to his plantation (eighteen miles) and divide the crop. I thought that this would give me an opportunity of witnessing the rich Southern planter in the splendor of his home surroundings. We reached the place just at sundown. It was a large one-story log house with the usual chimneys at each end of the outside and a broad piazza across the entire front, no better than the other planters' houses which I had visited. I at first thought it must belong to the overseer and made up my mind that if I was to be the guest of the overseer instead of the planter, they would learn before I was through with them that I was master, not servant. An old white-haired gentleman met us at the gate and was introduced by his son.

I found the house had but four rooms, all upon the first floor, with nothing overhead nearer than the shingled roof, the chairs all homemade with split bottoms, tableware of the cheapest kind, forks of iron, none of them ever having had more than two tines, and with knives [that] had evidently been in use for many generations, no carpets, nor in fact any evidence of splendor, luxury, or hardly comfort. I never afterwards attempted to find any realization of my boyhood fancies of Southern splendor.

In the early winter the Freedmen's Bureau sent me two female teachers from New Orleans. I was expected to levy and collect a tax from the people for the support of the schools. But I discovered that instead of strengthening my position the government was curtailing my powers, ordering my men back to their regiment, and leaving me with only two orderlies to govern the parish. I knew that to establish and compel the people to support and protect the colored schools would be beyond my power. I so informed the teachers and sent them back to Shreveport. One of them, an elderly woman, was much displeased, and commenced addressing me as general, an unexpected promotion; but at the end of three days, when she left, she had reduced me through all of the different grades downward to plain "Mister"—I think the most rapid case of promotion and reduction our army every knew.

Only a short time after this I was informed that civil government was to take the place of military government in the parish and was directed to recommend men for appointment to the civil positions. I recommended Unionists as the proper persons to receive these appointments, an idea which seemed to be concurred in by the ex-Confederates as well as the appointing power. In a short time the government was turned over to these new officers, while I retained only the agency of the Freedmen's Bureau, which gave me authority to act for the freedmen in any place where I thought their interest required it.

I had for a number of months been in full charge of the parish, at a time when a perfect change in the different relations of the people had taken place. Master, overseer, and slave had passed away, and all were legally on a perfect equality. This revolution I had successfully conducted in such a manner that the parish, before or since, has never seen an equal period of time so free from violence and crime.

I felt much relieved upon turning the government over to the civil officers but did not then, as now, fully realize the greatness and importance of the work performed. With the advent of civil government, satisfying the people that they were not to be punished for treason, social festivities commenced, the schools opened, and all went to work with renewed energy.

14

Adele Coleman, 1866

With the opening of the Sparta Academy came a Miss Coleman from the eastern portion of the parish as music teacher, boarding at the hotel where I took my meals. She had been carefully educated at the female college in Columbia, South Carolina, and as a lady was much superior to anyone whom I had seen in the country, a recognized belle, and a perfect sample of the Southern style of beauty.

It was not long before I discovered that the brass buttons and shoulder straps, so attractive to all feminine eyes, were having an effect upon her, notwithstanding that it was the uniform she had been taught to hate. Some of her admirers noticed earlier than I did that the Yankee captain was likely to be a dangerous rival. This and perhaps other causes had decided me to adopt the custom of the country and always go armed.

We were walking one evening in the large yard surrounding the house. She was so inattentive to what I was saying that, slightly piqued, I proposed to her that we go back to the house. Without in the least noticing my remark, but with flashing eyes she asked me for my revolver. Hesitatingly I handed it to her, stepping nearer so that I could catch her hand if I was the one she intended to use it upon. With a rapidity indicative of a full knowledge of its use and too quick for me to prevent her, she fired into the shrubbery by the fence. The second shot went into the air as I wrenched the revolver from her hand, and a young man jumped from the place and ran away. We walked back to the house, she remarking that she would teach him better than to eavesdrop on her, and then bid me good-night with scarcely any trace of excitement in her manner.

I have since learned enough of the customs and ideas of the Southern people to know that had she hit the young man, it would have been pronounced an accident. He, a young man of one of the first families, could not have been so dishonorable as to have been eavesdropping, while she could not have intentionally shot him. A certain pride and honor were of more importance than life to them.

This incident had the effect of placing one disgruntled suitor outside of speaking terms with Miss Coleman, and he immediately revenged himself by informing her parents that she was openly receiving the attentions of the Yankee officer at Sparta. He rightly judged that this would not be tolerated. The daughter of a family of South Carolina Huguenot stock,[1] her brothers both ex-officers of the Confederate army, the family connections being all large slaveholders, [she] must never bring a Yankee Puritan into the family. Consequently, in a few days Miss Coleman's brother came to take her home.

That night, as we passed out of the dining room, she handed me a letter written in a state of excitement which excused reserve, informing me that on account of a rumor having reached her parents that she was receiving marked attention from the Yankee officer at Sparta, she had been promptly ordered home. That night I answered her letter, enclosing my photograph, and handed them to her as we met at breakfast. It was soon known all over the parish that Miss Coleman had returned home and was being closely guarded to keep her from seeing the Yankee captain. Up to this time I had looked upon the matter only as a pleasant pastime; but with her it had evidently become a serious matter, while for the entire parish it was the subject of interest, talk, and speculation.

Her class (the old slaveholders), with but two prominent exceptions, approved of the course of the parents. Those two, looking farther into the future, said that with the changed order of things— their young men not being taught to work and the slaves free— Miss Coleman might do worse than marry the Yankee.

Brush Valley, Miss Coleman's home, was eighteen miles from Sparta, but we at once established a regular triweekly mail route,

1. Coleman is an English or Scottish name; it was Adele's mother, Judy, who claimed Huguenot descent. Also, the family lived in Mississippi before moving to Louisiana.

the courier always making his trips in the night, as he and his mule had to work in the field during the day.

I learned from some of my Masonic friends that a few hot-headed young men had been giving expression to the idea that it was her brother's duty to settle the question by shooting me on sight. This had the effect of keeping me thoroughly armed and always on my guard.

One night about ten o'clock the orderly came to my door and said that there was a young man outside who wanted to see me. I replied tell him to come in. The orderly returned, saying that the young man would not dismount but insisted on my coming out; and then in a low tone he added, "Captain, I would not go. He is mounted upon a fine white horse, acts very suspiciously, and will not allow me to come near him." Cocking my revolver, I slipped it into the breast of my coat, keeping my hand upon it in such a manner that I thought I could shoot first, and walked out. So apprehensive was I, under repeated warnings of an attempt to assassinate me, that at the raising of a hand or the slightest suspicious motion, I should have fired.

I advanced near enough to see what I thought was a smooth-faced boy and imperatively asked, "What do you want?" For my reply I received, "Marshall, don't you know me?" My hand dropped from my revolver while I stepped up to her horse and exclaimed, "My God, Adele, what brought you here at this time and in this shape?" She said, "Get your horse and ride back home with me, and I can tell you on the way."

Ordering my horse and telling the orderly that I was going out to a plantation some miles from town with the young man, we started. As soon as we passed out of town, Miss Coleman asked me if I had seen her brother Gus, adding that he left home early in the morning for the purpose of going to Sparta with some friends of his, intending to draw me into some dispute in which I might be shot and [he would] have plenty of witnesses present to furnish testimony that the shooting was in self-defense. Upon hearing this, she immediately had her horse saddled to visit a lady friend. There, with her friend's assistance, she secured a revolver and a suit of boy's clothing. As soon as it began to grow dark she took the road for her eighteen-mile ride to Sparta. Upon meeting people she rode with such speed that there was no time for recognition.

The last six miles of this journey was through a pine forest with but one house on the road.

Just as day was breaking, she requested me to stop in the road while she drove into the woods. In a few moments, in place of the boy who disappeared riding astride of his horse, appeared a young lady sitting with equal firmness upon her saddle. In half an hour I bid her good morning at her father's gate. A rapid ride of two hours and I was at home for breakfast and then to sleep.

Lieutenant Coleman [Gus] changed his mind after leaving home and did not start for Sparta until after his sister had left, as he learned from Miss Gray that she had gone there. While I was sleeping he was in town looking around to find his sister. He fell in with some of my friends who convinced him that it would be best to see me unarmed, that there would be plenty of time and opportunity to get arms if they were needed. He had met the old Vermont Brigade, to which I belonged, at Lee's Mills and upon various fields of battle in Virginia up to the time we captured him and a large portion of his brigade at Rappahannock Station, and I presume that he and others felt that if they desired, they could have a fight out of me more honorable than one in the street.

As soon as I was up an ex-Confederate captain and mutual friend came in and said that Mr. Coleman wanted to see me. He came in as others left the room and inquired where his sister was. I told him that at daybreak I left her at her father's door. He then rapidly asked a number of questions and inquired whether I was going to steal her without her parents' consent or what I was going to do, saying that the present state of affairs could not remain, that there must be a change someway. I replied that I should not marry his sister nor steal her against her wishes. Outside of that, I should make no promises further than to say that I should treat her honorably; that although the law of Louisiana still placed her under her parents' control, the laws of my state recognized her of age, she having passed eighteen; and that I had no very great respect for any of the statutes of a state one-half of which had to be set aside by military authority to make them accord with the present age of civilization. He immediately left my office for home. The next night our negro courier tapped on my window and handed me a long letter from Miss Coleman, from which I learned the result of the family consultation after her brother reached home.

First they attempted to coax, then to hire, and finally to drive her to go to South Carolina and cease her correspondence with me. She was positive in her refusals and threatened that if I was not permitted to visit her at the house, she would make no promise that she would not take another moonlight ride to Sparta. Finally, her positiveness drew from them the consent to invite me to visit her. I had heard at different times of remarks made by the family, the truth of which I did not doubt, indicating my inferiority as a Yankee plebeian to the Southern chivalry. I immediately replied that so much had been said and done that the invitation must come from the mistress of the house, her mother. The second day, the courier returned with a proper invitation, it being the first time he had made his trip by daylight. The next day, dressed in a civilian suit, I visited the Coleman mansion. I look back with great amusement to the careful and studied efforts [of] Mistress Coleman and myself to express to each other the dislike we felt without being exactly impolite or uncivil.

Before our marriage, which occurred some weeks later, I became considerably attached to Adele's father,[2] whom I found to be a man of good information and with very broad and liberal views, being one of the many in the South who considered the war unnecessary and uncalled for, saying that there would have been plenty of time to have resorted to arms and to have fought under the old flag after the Lincoln government had attempted to interfere unconstitutionally with Southern property rights. He, in my opinion, correctly divined that had that been done, a divided North and a solid South would have averted war.

On the 24th of July at early twilight, it was settled that we should be married at Mr. Coleman's house. Adele desired me to wear my uniform, as she wished all to understand that she was marrying a Yankee officer.

In the morning a violent storm of thunder, lightning, wind, and rain until noon made my anticipated ride of eighteen miles prospectively unpleasant. The last half of the day was as bright and

2. Isaac Coleman was evidently a member of the planter gentry, but it is difficult to be precise because of gaps in the historical records, especially the Federal Manuscript Census for Bienville Parish. He does not appear in the 1850 census, probably because he still lived in Mississippi, where Adele was born. The vital 1860 census for the parish was, alas, never made. An Isaac Coleman appears in the 1870 census, but the descriptive data—location in the parish, names and ages of his family members, property—fail to match what is known of Adele's father.

pleasant as could have been wished. About three p.m. I started with my orderly for Brush Valley. In my absentmindedness I missed my road, and at the time when I should have been at the house, I was several miles away. An hour late, with my horse foaming from the rapid ride, I arrived just in time to prevent the breaking up of the party, with most serious results to Adele. She was much too proud and in earnest to have accepted desertion and lived.

The marriage at once took place. The large parlor was perfectly lighted, windows and curtains up, the room filled with the white friends of the family, while around the windows, as far out in the darkness as we could see, were crowds of happy negroes from all the surrounding country. Standing in the centre of the room was the minister, Adele, dressed in the purest white, and by her side that Yankee uniform, so loved by the duskies on the outside and so hated by those inside.

Just before my marriage I received orders to turn over my office to an officer of the Veteran Reserve Corps[3] and report at New Orleans to be mustered out of the service. It was my intention, after stopping a few days with my father-in-law, to take my wife and go North by way of New Orleans. This soon became known and greatly to my surprise met with earnest opposition from all members of the family. After their arguments had been exhausted without the effect of shaking my previous plans, Mrs. Coleman informed me that Adele was threatened with consumption to such an extent that to take her North, she believed, would hasten her death. Upon this presentation of the case, much to the joy of the family, I started for New Orleans alone, riding the black Morgan horse, so unlike any other in the country, which I had brought with me. The day was intensely hot, and when I reached Coushatta my horse was ruined. This town then had but one building, a kind of storehouse. I little dreamed then that I would soon build an important town there and that the tragedy and horror with which I should be connected would make it one of the widest known in the South.

Upon my arrival at New Orleans I found a letter from my mother

---

3. Composed of men physically unfit for combat; originally called the "Invalid Corps."

in Vermont detailing property troubles, which decided me to go home before I returned to north Louisiana; and writing a letter to Adele, I left for the North. Not thinking of the change of temperature, I left my overcoat and had two or three severe chills during the week that I was at home. Business was soon completed and I was glad to be on my way to a warmer climate to spend the winter. When I reached Sparta I thought I detected a little surprise at my appearance. This was explained a little later when one of my friends told me in confidence that it was the general belief in the country that I had deserted my wife. I should have immediately started for Brush Valley, but my horse was in such a condition from its forty-mile travel of that day that I feared he would not last eighteen miles farther.

The next day just before noon, I rode up to Mr. Coleman's. The little negroes commenced hollering, "Captain Twitchell has come!" jumping, turning handsprings, and acting like as many wild people, quarrelling about who should carry in my saddlebags and who take care of my horse. No white family could have been more pleased at my arrival.

Adele showed by her looks that the prophesies of the busybodies in the country had had their effect upon her. I had fully made up my mind on my wife's account to stop in the South.

My duties had led me into different sections of the country, giving me an acquaintance more thorough in one year than a person staying at home would acquire in a lifetime. Brush Valley, I had learned, was far from being the best portion of the country. Mr. Coleman and myself decided to look around before I bought [land]. Starting on horseback we visited the Ouachita and Bayou Bartholomew valleys and then crossed the Mississippi to the state of Mississippi, finally around into Arkansas to the house of Miss Coleman, an old maid relative, who wanted I should come there, take her property, and look after her. There were many things in this ride unlike anything else I had ever known. Through my old travelling companion I gained a good insight into Southern customs. We rode up to a fine house one day [and] found no one at home but the negroes. Mr. Coleman at once ordered supper, it seemed to me, taking possession of the house in the most unwarranted manner. About dark the people returned [and] did not seem in the least surprised or annoyed by the liberty taken. In all our

journeys no offer to pay for entertainment was made except when
we stopped at hotels. Just before we reached Miss Coleman's in
Arkansas, the mule which I was riding died, and I was compelled
to hire a horse for the last few miles, a boy ten or twelve years old
coming on with us to take the horse back.

I found at Miss Coleman's the Methodist minister and his wife
of that circuit. He was [as] large and silent as she was small and
talkative, both inveterate smokers. Their peculiarities taxed my
self-control to the uttermost. From their conversation I learned
that they were travelling through their circuit both riding upon
one horse. Her ambition seemed to be the possession of a "critter"
of her own to ride.

Like many Southern places the house was enclosed by a fence,
and this enclosed again by a second fence. In this outside yard the
stock was corralled at night. In the morning I noticed a herd of
cattle in front of the house, among which was a fine Durham bull.
The boy who came with us was getting ready to return home.
Miss Coleman said to me you had better give the boy a quarter
and tell him to take his critter home. I had paid the boy for the use
of his horse and imagined that she meant to have him drive the
bull home and that I was to give the quarter to him for that purpose. So I walked out to the boy, told him to take the creature and
go on home. He looked at me a little scared but said nothing. I was
very positive that he should take it and start. They saw from the
piazza that something was wrong, and Mr. Coleman came out. I
then discovered that the "critter" meant was the horse which the
boy was leading, and although much annoyed at the time, I think
the pleasure that my mistake gave to the old people fully made up
for my annoyance.

I finally decided to purchase a plantation on Lake Bistineau.
The Colemans had so changed their views in reference to me that
they determined to purchase the adjoining plantation and run the
two to a certain extent together. Mr. Coleman and myself went to
New Orleans, he introducing me to his old commission merchant
with instructions to give me, in addition to my own credit, all
that he would give him. From this time on, all financial business,
hiring and discharging of hands, was left to me. The management
of the crops, of which I knew nothing, was left to the Colemans.

The few months we had to wait before we took possession of

the plantation I thought I would utilize and make profitable by going into the moss business in New Orleans with a man who had experience but not enough capital. Before I got through with it, capital and experience came very near changing places. I lost half what I was worth, but gained an experience in partnership affairs which has been of much service to me since.

15

Planting and Politics in
Bienville Parish, 1867–1869

Our first year's crop was poor, although better than any around us. Mr. Coleman was discouraged and, not being able to meet his obligations, seemed to be inclined to give up everything. Mrs. Coleman said to me one day, "You Yankees are said to be awful cute; seems to me you might take Mr. Coleman's business and straighten it out." I replied that if I was given absolute control and they would all do as I directed, it could be done. Everything was at once placed in my hands. My plan was to get rid of some land which he [Coleman] did not need. By a little management which they thought extremely shrewd, I in one week succeeded in making the sale, putting us financially above water again. After this time I bought and sold without hardly ever consulting anyone. As a sample of my purchases I bought 400 acres of land for $1,500 and leased it for a portion of the crops, my portion of which for the first year paid for the land. My success seemed to give everybody a desire to deal with me; consequently, all the opportunities for making money in the country were put in my way.

My first year's planting was during the government of the state before Reconstruction. I was appointed road overseer. At my last road working, when I dismissed the hands for the year, I informed them that they (the colored men) would be allowed to vote and that when that time came, they would be in great danger from two extreme parties. One party would put them back in slavery if they could; the other would crowd them forward into position so much faster than their education and experience in affairs of government would justify that the injury would be nearly as great.

The following summer, under the Reconstruction Act, registrars were appointed by General Sheridan[1] and sent up from New Orleans to register the voters of the parish, black and white, and hold an election for a member to a constitutional convention. The supervisors of registration sent up were not lacking educational qualifications, but with the exception of the chairman, they reflected no credit upon the appointing power nor honored in any way their positions.

The chairman soon made himself acquainted with me and at the same time with the character of his associates, who could not be brought to look upon the registering of negroes as anything serious or important, taking anything for a name which their love for fun and the negroes' ignorance might give them. In looking over the roll after it was completed, I found that they had registered one [freedman] as Alexander the Great and another as Jeremiah the Prophet. It was so late that the only remedy I could apply was to have the "the" stricken out from each name. The negroes all presented themselves for registration; the white people also generally registered.

As the time for the election approached, there seemed to be a general feeling of doubt in the minds of black and white about the kind of man who should be selected to represent the parish.[2] It was finally decided by the white people that to at once put at rest the question of their loyalty, they would vote for me, with the idea that the authorities would be perfectly satisfied and that as I had married and was living there, the best interests of the country would be my interests as well as theirs, while very naturally the colored men all desired to vote for me. I was nominated by J. H. Scheen, a prominent merchant of Sparta, there being no objection to my nomination in the mass meeting. I was two weeks in making up my mind, after the committee waited on me, that I would accept the nomination, and it was only from the representations that I was the only man in the parish upon whom all the different elements would unite that I accepted. The nomination was accepted with a prepared schoolboy speech which I presume gratified my hearers most when they discovered that I was through.

A young man, the editor of the parish paper and a rejected lover

1. Major General Philip H. Sheridan, commander of the Fifth Military District (Louisiana and Texas).
2. At the state constitutional convention mandated by the Reconstruction Acts.

of Adele's, came out as my opponent, saying that he thought I ought not to have all the good things; but he received only a few votes.

Raised in the state of Vermont where political excitement never runs high, of democratic parentage, I was at the time of my election perfectly independent. The question did not occur to me that it was in the least necessary for me to be a partisan, and had the question been asked whether I was a Democrat or Republican, I could not have answered.

The unreconciled Confederate element generally abstained from taking any prominent part in the election of delegates to the constitutional convention; consequently, the meeting of the convention showed its composition to be old Unionists, ex-Federal soldiers, and negroes of all complexions, from the bright octoroon to the full-blooded negro. With the exception of a few of the last class, all were very well fitted for their position. The Unionists were especially rich in men of experience, education, and ability. The ex-Federal soldiers with their Northern ideas of government were a very necessary balance between the two factions.

As one of the youngest men of the convention, I took an active part only upon the question that the school moneys of the state should be expended for the education of the children and that the system heretofore practised, of allowing the parents to deduct the school allowance from their taxes and then educate their children or not, should be done away with. I was very much surprised when I returned home to find that this act had made me very unpopular with the white people, who rightly looked upon it as a distinctly Northern idea.

After about one hundred days, the convention adopted the constitution, March 7, 1868, and provided for its being committed to the people [for ratification] on the 17th and 18th days of April following. Immediately after the adoption of the constitution by the convention, the Republicans met and nominated officers. I represented Bienville in the nominating convention, my first party action, taken for the reason that I found all elements there friendly to the Union and all accepting the results of the war.

After [my] returning to the parish, the Republican candidates for parish officers were nominated. I took the head of the ticket as parish judge; Edward W. Dewees, another ex-Federal, [was nominated] as representative to the legislature; [the nominees for]

Marshall Harvey Twitchell at about age thirty. Courtesy of Dr. Marshall Coleman Twitchell.

Adele Coleman Twitchell. Courtesy of Dr. Marshall Coleman Twitchell.

Marshall Harvey Twitchell, probably in the consulate in Kingston. Courtesy of Dr. Marshall Coleman Twitchell.

Marshall Harvey Twitchell in his tailored Civil War uniform, *ca.* 1900. Courtesy of Dr. Marshall Coleman Twitchell.

Marshall Harvey Twitchell, Henrietta Day Twitchell, and their sons
Emmus George (upper left) and Marshall Coleman (upper right), *ca.* 1900.
Reproduced from a photograph in the Twitchell Family Papers, courtesy of the
University of Vermont Library.

clerk, recorder, sheriff, justices of the peace, and constables [were] all Union men. On account of Northern birth, army record, and Southern marriage, I could better control the different elements of the party than anyone else and was consequently given the entire election management with an absoluteness never allowed in the Northern states, for which my army experience fitted me.

My wife's people used every argument possible to have me withdraw from the campaign. While I had no particular taste for the responsibilities and work of the leadership which was thrust upon me, upon canvassing the matter, I found that my withdrawal would break up the party. The colored people wanted a Northern man for their leader. The Unionists would obey no other Northern man in the parish.

I was informed by Judge Head,[3] a friend of mine and the most influential man in the other party, that they would contest the election and that they expected to be able to defeat our entire ticket. As the campaign advanced I learned from different sources, enough to satisfy me, that the contest would be so close that success would be gained only by the hardest work, closest attention, and best of management. In looking back I do not know how our management could have been better.

The week before the election I visited different portions of the parish, speaking to large crowds every day. My meetings were held at places ten or fifteen miles apart. I made the trip on an old mule, too slow to be of much use in the field, which used to vary the monotony of the journey by occasionally falling on its knees. When my feet and the mule's nose struck the ground, it would immediately rise and go on again as though nothing had happened.

During this political campaign the Ku Klux organization appeared with its murders and outrages.[4] Moses Langhorne, a promi-

3. J. R. Head, editor of the *Rural Times.*
4. Twitchell has become confused here about the chronology of events probably because there were two important elections in 1868. On April 17 and 18 was the special election of a Reconstruction government and the referendum on the new constitution. Seven months later, in November, was the Grant-Seymour presidential election. The spring election witnessed incidents of fraud and intimidation in the Red River valley that resulted (as Twitchell relates) in appeals before the state board of registration in New Orleans. Still, by the standards of the era, this first Reconstruction election in the state was comparatively peaceful.

The presidential election was another matter. Stunned by the Republican victory in April, Louisiana whites turned to wholesale assassination and terror to win the state for Democrat Horatio Seymour. Moreover, while the spring cam-

nent colored man, was murdered in his house by masked men, his head cut from his body and taken away. Asa Shehea, a bright young mulatto who was acting as my political messenger, disappeared. It was reported that his hands and feet were tied, and then he was dropped into Lake Bistineau. These murders, with various whippings of prominent colored men in different portions of the parish, had such effect that upon the first day of the election I discovered the success of our ticket was extremely doubtful. The great fight was made against me, as the leader of the Republican party in the parish, and Dewees, we being the only ones who could influence the negro vote. Dewees was much the weakest one on the ticket.

The Democrats had nominated against me, largely through my secret influence, their most popular man, but one whom I knew was ineligible. The adoption of the constitution and the election of a Republican governor would result in preventing the issuing of commissions to any candidates who were under disability; the votes for such a candidate would be declared blank.[5]

During the night of the first day [of the election], I sent a messenger to Dewees at Sparta, telling him my fears and instructing him to trade off votes for me wherever he could gain for himself. I vigorously pursued the same policy at Ringgold. The result was that the entire ticket was elected by a small majority, excepting Dewees and myself. We quickly secured enough evidence of illegal votes to secure Dewees' election, and he went on to New Orleans to secure his seat in the legislature and file evidence of Head's ineligibility. Head was the acting parish judge at the time of the election, a just officer, a good man, and as I had no particu-

---

paign lasted only a few weeks, the violence preceding the presidential election went on for six long months, beginning in May only a few weeks after the April balloting. Thus over the years the two campaigns blurred in Twitchell's mind into a single episode. The savage violence he describes—the murder of Moses Langhorne, the disappearance of Asa Shehea, the attack on W. H. Honnus, and presumably the ostracism—all this occurred after the April election, not before.

As to the Ku Klux Klan, it was rumored to be active throughout Louisiana in 1868. Hard evidence of its existence, however, is scanty, leading Joe Gray Taylor to doubt that it ever existed in the state as a formal organization (*Louisiana Reconstructed, 1863–1877* [Baton Rouge, 1974] 162). On the other hand, the existence of the Knights of the White Camellia is not a matter of speculation; this Klan-like organization was the main instrument of white terror in Louisiana that year.

5. The Reconstruction Acts and the new Louisiana constitution disfranchised Southerners who had voluntarily aided the Confederacy.

lar desire for the position, I took no steps to hurry him out. I felt that it would be quite as well for all concerned that he should learn for himself that he could not qualify for the office; that his election was a nullity; that under the constitution just adopted, the governor would fill the place by appointment, [and] that his competitor would be the appointee.

A few weeks after the election, [the Democratic] party committee returned from a visit to New Orleans and informed the people that they had lost all of the offices which they might have held; that their candidate for parish judge was ineligible and that I would be appointed in his place; that the legislature was strongly Republican and Dewees would get his seat. There was much abuse of their party leaders, who by their outrages had gained for the parish a bad reputation and then had not been successful, while our undisguised friendship and activity for each other had taught them that Dewees and I had no disagreement about the election, and my apparent desire to prevent the nomination of a competitor who was beaten was well known to all.

Smarting from the stings of conscience for murders committed, wounded in pride for being outwitted, they determined to terrorize, murder, or drive out the Republican leaders. Union men, having been humbled during the Confederacy, they did not think would require extreme measures.

Just before the election, W. H. Honnus, a Northern man and ex-Federal soldier, moved into the parish from New Orleans. He leased a plantation two miles west of me and commenced planting. One evening after dark he was called to his gate, ostensibly to receive a letter, and was shot within a few feet of his supposed friends and neighbors, each one of the party shooting at him (so that all might be equally guilty), his wife screaming meanwhile for them to stop.[6]

A short time after I had retired that night, a party called at my gate for me to come out and get a letter. I hurriedly dressed, strapped on my revolver, took my carbine, and softly passed out of the back door round to the front, where I could command the front door, while my wife sent out a little negro girl for the letter.

6. Honnus had been a supervisor of registration and the Republican candidate for parish sheriff in the April election. Twitchell's testimony about the attack on him appears in *House Miscellaneous Documents*, 41st Cong., 2nd Sess., No. 154, Pt. 1, p. 62.

They had lost the letter and rode away without being recognized by the girl. Hardly had they disappeared when a trusty negro informed me that Honnus had been shot, was helpless but not dead, and that Mrs. Honnus wanted me to come at once, as she feared they would return, kill her, her child, and finish her husband.

As one of the effects of slavery, the negroes had a perfect network of trails between the different plantations, which they could follow without the least danger of interception from the travelled road. Telling Ben to take the trail, I followed him back to Honnus' house. Honnus had, with the help of his wife, crawled into the house and upon the bed. A quick examination proved that although he had a dozen or more wounds, they were all superficial; the only bone broken was in the hand. A negro was sent with a written note to Dr. Jones of Ringgold to come out and dress Honnus' wounds. I also sent out word that I intended to stay with Mr. Honnus with my carbine, which I felt certain would be sufficient to prevent any attack upon a wounded man by those who had only sufficient courage to shoot an unarmed man in the dark. The doctor came and dressed his wounds, which proved to be troublesome but none of them serious.

During the day, I selected three negroes whom I thought would be best for the purpose to be nearby with their shotguns to assist me in case of an attack. Just before dark my wife rode up with her revolver and informed me that she would stay if I did. I knew too much of her positive character to object, while I had seen enough of her nerve and familiarity with firearms to feel that she was a greater reinforcement than half a score of some men would be.

That night a negro picket was stationed on the road [on] each side of the house, while we guarded the entrance. The next day Honnus and his family decided to abandon their growing crop and return to New Orleans. There was no further danger of an attack upon the family, and we were relieved from our guard duty. In a few days Honnus and his family moved to the city.

About this time an attempt was made to socially ostracize me and, by sending anonymous letters to my wife, to create trouble between us. This last act had just the opposite effect from the one desired. The social customs and amusements of the country were so disagreeable to me that to be relieved of any part of them was a positive pleasure. Upon our first appearance at church after this plan had been decided upon, the minister aimed his whole discourse at my wife for having married one from outside of her people. I found the sermon so rich in political material that I commenced taking notes. This was soon observed and in some manner the speaker's attention was called to it, causing him to stop short in an address which to me was very interesting and amusing. Owing to the social standing of my wife's family, the ostracism gradually fizzled out.

As milder methods did not affect me, the public was prepared by the customary stories (sometimes that I was killed and at others that I would be) for my assassination. I learned of all their stories, as they much preferred that I should be frightened out of the parish; for if they could satisfy the Republicans that their leaders were cowards, that party would soon fall to pieces.

About midsummer I received letters from Dewees to the effect that he could not sufficiently prove some outrages which were committed on the day of the election near Arcadia (twenty-five miles from where I lived), and if I could not get the testimony, he would lose his seat.

The taking of my life would be considered a very small matter in the minds of the Democrats if it prevented this testimony from reaching the city. I started from home at midnight and reached Freedmansville early in the morning, much to the surprise of the scared negroes who flocked out to see me. I ordered one to rub down and feed Wicked Bill; then taking the witnesses into a house, I took their testimony by virtue of my position as justice of the peace, which I had long held. In the afternoon I rode into Sparta on my way home, stopped, and by my remarks and actions indicated that I intended to stay all night in town.

My appearance here, coming in an opposite direction from my home, was of course a surprise. I knew the chivalry well enough to know that after dark they would receive reinforcements from different localities and from the grocery, and that I would then be in great danger. Just about dark I brought my horse up to the crowded steps of the store and remarked that it was so comfortable I thought I had better ride on to Rabun's (a Union family eight miles from Sparta) for the night. Their displeased looks were their only reply. I walked my horse out of the village and then for eight miles took that rapid gallop which only the mustang can long endure. Just before bedtime I reached Rabun's, took tea, and immediately started for home, eleven miles distant. At midnight my journey was ended, with my object accomplished. I had ridden fifty miles, much of the distance during the night, taken three affidavits, and created any amount of excitement in the past twenty-four hours.

Between Rabun's and Ringgold the road runs through a brushy swamp, where it was supposed I must pass in the morning. That road was carefully picketed, and so certain were they that I would be killed they sent a dispatch from the nearest telegraph station that Captain Twitchell had been in Sparta the day before and left for home late in the evening; his horse had reached home with blood upon the saddle but without the rider, and it was feared that the captain had been assassinated by some of his personal enemies. In a few days I had the pleasure of reading my own obituary, written in the customary "all virtue and no faults" style, in the New Orleans *Republican.*

Towards night the next day, individuals both black and white commenced calling. To the surprise of all, chagrin of some, and pleasure of others, they were able to see the man all thought dead. The supposed inconsolable widow was in the highest spirits, which naturally followed the hours of depression while I was absent on my dangerous trip. No one seemed to have the courage to ask if I had been away from home. My father-in-law's people did not know that I had been gone; the few negroes who were aware of the fact promptly replied that they did not know I had been away.

Fifteen miles from Sparta there was a strong Union settlement known as the Jones neighborhood. These people, during the war, gave much trouble to the Confederacy, under the leadership of Tom Jones, one of those noble old Unionists who for three years endured the persecutions of the Rebels for a government which immediately ignored and neglected him as soon as it came to power. Jones had been our candidate for state senator. During my stop in Sparta I had so much to say about the Jones settlement and gave them so much apocryphal information about old Tom Jones that all were impressed with the idea that that was where I had been. Upon this false scent they commenced trying to find out where I had been, while I slipped away to New Orleans with my testimony before my visit to Freedsmanville, with its object, was discovered. The presentation of the testimony confirmed my friend Dewees in his seat; and when I had qualified before the secretary of state as parish judge in place of Head, who had been disqualified, I started for home.

Leaving the steamboat at Coushatta, I hired a mule for my twenty-five-mile ride, relying for my safety upon being in the country before I was expected. It did not occur to me then that the Knights of the White Camellia[7] in Coushatta would receive their orders to dispose of me when I landed. The little delay which was necessary to procure a mule was sufficient for them to get ahead of me and picket the road at a point in the wood twenty miles from my house. Just before reaching this wood, a road turned to the left, making a circuit of six miles [before] returning to the main road. Busy with my thoughts, I did not notice until it was too late to turn back that the mule had taken the left-hand road, thereby, as I afterwards learned, saving my life. Two years later one of these pickets became a warm friend and supporter of mine and informed me that they waited so long for me at that point that they saw it would be too late for them to overtake me before I was out of the jurisdiction of their lodge, so no further attempt was made that day.

I made formal demand upon Head for my office as parish judge. The demand was refused and the case fixed for trial before Judge Lewis in chambers at Minden. This place was twenty miles north of my home, with no public conveyance. I had made arrangements to start on horseback at midnight but was taken violently ill (an unusual thing for me) with an attack of bilious colic, and not being any better at daybreak, my wife sent a note to my lawyer requesting him to go on with the case, as I could not be there. The courier, mounted upon my horse, was soon on his way with the letter. While passing through a swamp, the man was stopped by a picket who inquired where Captain Twitchell was and why he was not going to Minden, saying to the colored man, "I came near shooting you off from that horse, which I know is Captain Twitchell's and I almost wish I had. It would have served you right for working for such a man."

My political success and many evasions of assassination in-

7. *Knights of the White Camellia* has been substituted here for *White League* because the White League was not created until 1874.

curred the bitterness of my enemies at the same time that it brought to my support the elements which always follow success.

In the fall came the exciting presidential election of 1868. The Republicans of the parish of Bienville were completely cowed and frightened. I was compelled to advise them to stay at home and make no attempt to vote, as I knew the lives of many of them would certainly be sacrificed if they did. I rode to Ringgold the day of the election, walked up to the ballot box, and voted an open ticket for Grant. That I was determined to vote was well known by the onlookers, who parted as if by some prearranged plan, leaving me space to walk for thirty feet through a mob of my political enemies. I did not hear a word spoken from the time I appeared until I left. I reached home in a few hours, much to the joy of my wife and mother-in-law; although the latter was an intense Democrat, it pleased her that they were not able to frighten me out of voting. Those familiar only with Northern election methods might criticize my advice to Republicans, thinking that others might have voted undisturbed as I did. I knew they could not, and although I would risk my own life, I did not think it right for me to sacrifice the lives of my friends. The parish, which had gone Republican by 150-vote majority in April, cast but one Republican vote in November;[8] 950 votes were suppressed.

During the war the navigation of Lake Bistineau, by the neglect of the state authorities, had become very much impaired, which was a matter of vital importance to Bienville and Claiborne parishes. A bill was introduced in the legislature in January, 1869, appropriating $50,000 for the clearing of the lake. Four men were named in the bill to perform the work; the measure was Democratic throughout. During the last stages of the bill, my friend Dewees secured the substitution of my name for one of the incorporators, the others being prominent Democratic politicians of Minden. The governor at first refused to sign the bill, plainly telling them [the measure's backers] that he felt very little interest in a community which had murdered his supporters and had by crime changed Republican into Democratic parishes. This news was

8. The one Republican vote was of course Twitchell's (*House Miscellaneous Documents*, 41st Cong., 2nd Sess., No. 154, Pt. 1, p. 62).

quickly taken to Minden. My brother-in-law appeared there the next day and purchased the interests of the different incorporators, who felt that they were getting money for something of no value until my drafts were given them in payment for their assignments when they began to doubt.

As soon as my agent had left, the town was filled with their boastings of how they had outwitted the Yankee. In a few days they learned that the governor had signed the bill;[9] their boastings ceased and their reputation for smartness disappeared. I at once employed a steamboat captain, himself interested in the navigation of the lake, to take charge of the work. It was pressed so faithfully during the summer as to surprise the inhabitants, who had always been accustomed to a lax expenditure of public moneys and an easy performance of public works.

The Democrats, discovering that faithful work would increase my political strength, determined to make the affair crush me financially, as the money was not to be paid by the state until the job was completed and accepted. I had borrowed quite a large sum, which I could not repay at the specified time if the state payment was delayed.

The best lawyer of the parish was sent to New Orleans to enjoin the payment of the money and get the matter into the courts, when they could easily delay the case until my ruin was completed. I learned of their plan and, by placing it before the state auditor, succeeded in getting him and the warrant clerks to work all night in the issuing of the warrants for my payment.

The next morning I saw the attorney, with whom I was well acquainted, and told him that I had heard what he was in the city for and I wished he would not do it. He replied, "I dislike to do it on account of your wife's family, but a lawyer must serve his employers." I then said, "The best reason I know for you not doing it is that you are six hours too late."

9. *Acts of the State of Louisiana,* 1870, p. 6 (the governor signed it too late for inclusion in the 1869 volume).

16

Starlight Plantation and
Red River Parish, 1869–1871

In the spring of 1869 my father-in-law, not satisfied with the new system of labor, placed all of his plantation interests in my charge. This, taken in connection with the Lake Bistineau improvements, kept me exceedingly busy. By getting rid of some unprofitable real estate and making good crops, I was in condition to purchase Starlight Plantation, a very valuable place on the Red River near Coushatta Point, [from Colonel C. K. Gillespie.]

After purchasing, I learned that the plantation belonged to Colonel Gillespie's wife and children, and it became necessary for me to buy the place at a sheriff's sale in order to perfect the title. This was done as soon as the proper orders could be obtained from court; I bid the price agreed upon, $21,000—$7,000 to be paid the first of next May and the remainder in one or two years. I became thoroughly impressed with the idea that Colonel Gillespie (an ex-Confederate) was a rogue before the transactions were all completed, and had been correspondingly cautious in making out the papers and taking receipts. At the same time, I had been very careful that the colonel should not discover how much I doubted his oft-repeated declarations of honesty; in fact, my first suspicion arose from his professing too much friendship.

During this summer my only brother Homer and my brother-in-law George A. King joined me from Vermont. I employed them upon the lakes until the work was completed and then sent them to Starlight to look after my interests and prepare for the coming year while the previous owner was moving away.

In December, while in the city making preparations for the coming year's work, I was surprised to receive a letter from my brother saying that the ginhouse (where the lint of the cotton was separated from the seed) had been burned under suspicious circumstances and that Colonel [Gillespie] had started for the city. I soon learned that the building was insured and that he was there to collect the insurance. In this I found he was too quick for me; consequently, I accepted his promise that he would adjust the insurance in May.

Early in 1870 Colonel Gillespie and his family moved, and I was in full possession of Starlight. The house was at first saddened by the death of my only son Harvey. He had always been very frail, and the miasma of the Red River proved too much for his strength.

I found that among my plantation hands there were many abundantly able to manage the field part of the plantation work, and I was left with my brother and King comparatively free to carry out the intended improvements. New machinery with steam power for cotton gin, sawmill, and gristmill was at once brought up from the city, to the value of nearly $5,000, this being the first that had been brought into the country since the war.

Before the year was out, the machinery was all in position in a large two-story building, and a new dwelling house erected near it for Mr. King, to whom I gave the management of the mill. I also built a schoolhouse and eight new houses for the negroes, considerably improving the old system of negro quarters. The change most noticeable was that they were placed in different portions of the plantation instead of in one cluster, as in slavery times. This removed the cause of a great many disagreements among the hands, placed them nearer their work, and gave me an opportunity to hold each head of family responsible for his portion of the plantation.

In April, much to my surprise, Colonel Gillespie called and informed me that he had purchased a plantation fifteen miles up the river upon which he must pay $10,000 down. After taking possession, he had discovered that he could not make out the $10,000 without I would advance him $3,000 on the second payment. He said the parties of whom he bought were desirous to get out of the trade, and unless the $10,000 in greenbacks or gold was paid on the second day of May, he would lose the place; and [he] asked me if I would be there on the day specified with that amount. I assured him that I would. From my own observation and inquiry, I had thoroughly learned the character of the man and determined that before he got any money not due him, he should first pay me for the ginhouse which he had burned.

On the morning of May 2, Mr. King, my brother Homer, and myself went up the river on horseback, our saddlebags filled with gold and greenbacks on one side and revolvers on the other, as I knew a careful preparation for difficulty was the only way to avoid one. It was late in the day before the business reached the point which required a payment of the money. There were quite a number of parties interested in the plantation, and each one was to receive the amount due him or her separately.

I commenced counting gold and small money until I reached the $7,000 due, then rose from the table, remarking that that was all I owed Colonel Gillespie. There was quite an excitement for a few moments, King and myself being apparently the only ones free from it. The colonel asked me if I did not promise to bring $10,000. I said yes, I had brought the money, but no arrangement had been made as yet about my paying it out, that the ginhouse matter would have to be settled before it was paid; and to shorten the transaction, I informed him that my action was premeditated and that we had come fully prepared for any emergencies that might arise. After an hour's squirming, he allowed me one-half of the money he had received from the insurance company for the ginhouse, which was the amount I had decided it was worth. Only those who are familiar with such kind of men can understand the marked respect with which Colonel Gillespie ever after treated me.

The month of June, I was engaged as deputy U.S. marshal in taking the census in the parish of De Soto, brother Homer having charge, for the same purpose, of the western half of Bienville Parish. On account of their ignorance the people required long explanations and sometimes a show of authority before they would answer questions. In one case my brother found only the wife and a large family of grown-up daughters at home. That night the man of the house with some of his neighbors, all armed with shotguns, came to Ringgold, where my brother was spending the night, and said he was hunting for young Twitchell, who had been at his house insulting his family. Fortunately, there were a few men in town of more intelligence, who, after learning that the "outrageous insults" to his daughters consisted in requiring of them their ages and writing it upon paper, persuaded the old man that his action for insult must be against the United States government, that young Twitchell was not to blame.

My duties in the South before this had always brought me in contact, almost entirely, with the old slaveholder and his former slaves; and I used to wonder that such a small number of people, as the ex-slaveholders were in proportion to the whole number, could have inaugurated and carried on a war which was directly against the interests of the slaves who had fed their army and the nonslaveholders who had filled its ranks. Before the 30th of June I had discovered ignorance enough to fully explain the question.

In the fall of 1870 the remainder of my father's family, including my mother, sister Helen and her husband, Monroe C. Willis, [sister] Katie and her husband, Clark Holland, joined me at Starlight. Sister Belle, the wife of George A. King, had come South in the spring. Work was quickly divided, Willis and King taking charge of the mills while brother Homer and Holland managed the plantation.

In the fall of this year I was elected to the state Senate from the senatorial district comprising the parishes of De Soto, Sabine, and Natchitoches, receiving nearly two-thirds of the 5,427 votes cast. Every parish gave a Republican majority. There was but little attempt at improper control of the voters. This was the last fair expression of the popular will which the district has ever known.

It had long been the desire of that portion of the country in which I lived that a new parish should be created out of portions of De Soto, Natchitoches, Bienville, and Bossier parishes. Legislative members had been elected upon that issue but had never been able to carry their point. It was well understood that I was favorable to the project. The largely Democratic northern portion of Natchitoches was strongly in favor of the new parish. Their committee waited upon me and an agreement was made: that I should make no speeches in that part of the country, for which they would give me the entire Democratic vote. [After the election,] I had a careful examination of the ballots made and found that they had given me thirteen votes. I immediately called on the chairman of the [Democratic] committee, showed him the figures, and informed him that I should be careful about ever again trading with those who would not or could not deliver the article traded. The desire for this trade was not on account of my ability as a speaker, nor do I think the Democrats favorable to the new parish feared my defeat; but the Southern Democratic party could no more then, than now, survive having the truth told to its voters.

On the first Monday in January [1871] I took my seat in the Louisiana Senate and at once commenced work pertaining to the parish of Red River. I soon discovered that the representatives from the parishes which would lose territory by the new bill were opposed to it for no other reason than that it made their parishes smaller. No attempt was made to answer the plea of inconvenience to the citizens under the present law; no claim [was made] against the justice and needs of the new law.

After becoming satisfied that I could not accomplish the passage of the act in an open manner, I resorted to the following ruse: The bill had passed the Senate and was in the House. Securing the services of a lawyer who was on good terms with the opponents of the bill in the House, I gave him an amendment which he represented to the House was one that would cause me to amend it again when it reached the Senate. It would then again have to go to the House, and in that way they would get the advantage of not having openly opposed the bill. The amendment was adopted and the bill came to the Senate, and three of the House members came in to see what I would do with the amendment. I called up the bill and moved that the Senate concur in the amendment. It was done and the Senate adjourned. The House members, surprised at the quickness with which the bill was disposed of and not understanding just what was its disposal, asked what I had done with the amendment. I told them that it was concurred in and the bill was passed, and to their surprise I informed them that I had written the amendment myself but presumed the lawyer did not tell them so. From this time on, Republicans of the 22nd district rarely differed in their views of questions before the legislature.

During the summer of 1871, in accordance with the act authorizing its creation, the new parish of Red River was organized. The first officers were appointed by the governor upon my recommendation. It has been one of the serious charges against me that I filled the offices with my carpetbag relatives, and for that reason I will give the record of the different parish officers, as this was the only set that I ever had the power to fasten upon the people;

after this first organization all officers but tax collectors were elected by the people:

    parish judge, A. O. P. Pickens, ex-Confederate officer
    parish attorney, T. E. Paxton, ex-Confederate officer
    clerk of court, Duke H. Hayes, ex-Confederate tax collector
    parish treasurer, Julius Lisso, ex-Confederate soldier
    sheriff, John T. Yates, Southern Unionist
    coroner, Andrew Bosley, colored
    recorder, Homer J. Twitchell, carpetbagger.

The tax collector [Stokes] who served for a short time, appointed by the governor without my recommendation, was a man of unknown previous record and the only one of the officers considered objectionable by either of the political parties. The objection came from his not being a resident of the parish at the time of his appointment. When these appointments came before the Senate for confirmation in the winter of 1872, in deference to the wishes of the parish for resident officers, Stokes's name was not sent in.

Immediately following the organization of the parish government, I took steps for the establishment of the public schools. I had received the hearty cooperation and assistance of all the people up to this time, but no one seemed desirous of assisting or having anything to do with the schools if the "niggers" could attend. I very soon discovered that this was a matter so serious that the schools must be given up entirely to the white children or that I must almost absolutely take charge of the matter and upon my own shoulders carry the responsibility of establishing schools which the colored children could attend. There was every reason that the schools should be open to the colored children. They were in a degraded state on account of their ignorance and were very desirous of attending. The school fund, which was raised by poll tax, was largely taken from the colored men on account of the black population being very much in excess of the white in the Red River valley. The only reason against their education was that the white people disliked to see the negro educated, a dislike which came entirely from the old system of slavery. After some delays in ineffectual attempts to satisfy the white people, I built a schoolhouse on Starlight and employed my sister Helen, one of the best of New England's teachers, to commence the school. I hoped by this course to sufficiently break down the prejudice against teaching colored schools so that I would be able to hire competent teachers.

The law required that the public schools should be open to all the children of the state, without regard to race or color.[1] To enforce the law in my section meant the closing of the schools or a continuous rebellion. I opened two schools in each ward in the parish. The people were informed that one school was for the white children and the other for the colored. The separation was made by common consent and, at that time, much to the advantage of both races.

I then heard the general talk was that the negroes would soon tire of learning, and lack of scholars would close the colored schools. Every month the attendance increased, and then came the repeated rumors that the colored schools were to be broken up and the [school]houses burned by the wild young men of the neighborhood. I waited as long as I thought prudent and then notified the people that the day the colored school in any neighborhood was broken up, that day I would withdraw the money from the white school in that district. People well understood that I made no idle threats, and all trouble in reference to the schools was at an end until Democratic government took possession of the state, when one of their first acts was to destroy the colored schoolhouse at Starlight.

With the organization of the government, the parish entered upon an era of prosperity unequalled in Louisiana, if not in the whole South. For the first time since the war, the laborer felt a degree of confidence that he would get the profits of his labor; consequently, the landowners had no difficulty in making improvements which it had been impossible for them to accomplish with dissatisfied labor. Old fields were taken in and new ones opened, cabins built and repaired. So great was the improvement that the passenger on the deck of the steamboat could quickly discern when he entered the parish of Red River. The town of Coushatta was built at Coushatta Point, courthouse and jail erected, and in three years, from a simple steamboat landing, Coushatta

1. Article 135 of the state constitution of 1868.

had become the third town in size and importance on the Red River.[2]

In two or three instances the Southern desperado made his appearance but was so quickly disposed of that the parish soon gained a reputation for law and order equalled only by its prosperity. I did not notice at that time that it was the carpetbaggers of the parish who always suppressed these bullies, but my after familiarity with the people gave me the reason. The Southerner raised among them had a certain fear for the half-drunk desperado loaded with revolvers and bowie knives. The carpetbagger had a contempt for him and naturally, when he first overstepped the bounds of law, was ready to seize him.

2. A boast confirmed by the 1872 survey of Samuel H. Lockett, no admirer of carpetbaggers (*Louisiana as It Is: A Geographical and Topographical Description of the State,* ed. Lauren C. Post [Baton Rouge, 1970], 67).

17

Election of 1872 and the Colfax Massacre

At the [April] election of 1868 the leading Democrats of the state abstained from voting or taking part in the election.[1] Their inordinate vanity and egotism led them to the belief that the state could not be governed without them. By 1872[2] they had discovered their mistake and made earnest endeavours to regain their lost power.

In New Orleans this resulted in the election of a strong Democratic delegation. In many instances the elections were disputed, and in others the candidate had resolved not to qualify according

1. This is a considerable exaggeration. While 66,152 Louisianians, most of them black, had voted for the constitution of 1868, 48,739 citizens, most of them white, had opposed it. The Democrats had nominated no candidate for governor, but many Democrats had supported conservative Republican James G. Taliaferro, who received nearly 39,000 votes.

2. *1872* has been substituted for *1870*. Since Twitchell accurately comments on the 1870 election in Chapters 16 and 19, the mistake here is perhaps an uncorrected typographical error.

Twitchell is confusingly brief about the background of these events. The Louisiana election of 1872 was bizarre. The all-important governor's race pitted Republican senator William Pitt Kellogg against Democrat John D. McEnery. The joker in the deck was incumbent Republican governor Henry Clay Warmoth, who defected to the Democrats and turned the Republican election apparatus against his own party. The result was a disputed election so confusing that no one has ever been able to tell who won. Both sides claimed victory, however, and acted accordingly. In the winter and spring of 1873 Louisiana had two governors, two legislatures, and in many parts of the state, two sets of parish officials. The crisis lasted until May, when President Ulysses S. Grant arbitrarily decided the conflict in favor of the Republicans.

The trouble at Colfax was directly related to the election. Both Republicans and McEneryites claimed control of Grant Parish. As tension mounted that spring, black farmers began gathering at Colfax for protection. On Easter Sunday, 1873, they were attacked by several hundred armed whites. Following the euphemism of Reconstruction, the massacre has usually been called the Colfax "Riot."

to the laws of the state. I was selected as chairman of the very important committee on elections,[3] perhaps on account of the old Vermont Brigade, of which I had been a member, and my insensibility to the dangers around me, which naturally came from my not knowing their existence. It took many a bitter and bloody lesson to teach me that the Southern Democrats considered murder and assassination legal political weapons.

In the Senate a party of newly elected extremists under the leadership of a little wizened-faced person by the name of [Benjamin Franklin] Jonas (Cleveland's[4] collector of customs at New Orleans in 1888) decided that they would not take the oath to support the constitution of the state, the constitution framed by men who had been loyal to the Federal government during the war while they, the people of Louisiana, were not represented.

A resolution was introduced expelling all senators who refused to take the oath; this was referred to my committee. The next morning I reported the resolution favorably and the second morning moved the adoption of the report, paying not the slightest attention to the scowls of the New Orleans thugs who filled the lobby of the Senate. Little Jonas never forgave me for not being frightened out of doing my duty and compelling him and his friends to take the proper oath.[5]

Fifty miles below Coushatta another new parish had been created, called the parish of Grant; the parish seat was Colfax. The officers of this parish were, some of them at least, of questionable character. This, taken in connection with their conduct, brought about a dispute which resulted, in April, 1873, in the besieging of a large party of colored people in the courthouse. Two white men were killed, and as appeared in the trial before the United States Court, the bodies of fifty-nine colored men were found. The num-

---

3. This is not entirely correct. Twitchell was a member of the senate committee on elections and was perhaps the real leader of the committee, but A. E. Barber (black) was chairman; Twitchell was chairman of the committee on auditing and supervising the expenses of the senate (*Louisiana Senate Journal*, extra session, December, 1872).

4. President Grover Cleveland.

5. Apart from the fact that Jonas was never seated in the senate, Twitchell's account of these events cannot be confirmed by the *Louisiana Senate Journal*; legislative journals, however, give only a skeletal outline of proceedings.

ber who were thrown into the river and crawled away into the swamp to die of their wounds must ever remain unknown.[6]

The following is from the New Orleans *Times*,[7] a Democratic paper, which would certainly not print anything darker than they believed was the truth. [The narrator is R. G. Hull of Marshall, Texas.]

> The trouble in Grant parish, La., came to a rather bloody termination last Sunday, 13th inst., and as I happened to be one of the passengers on the steamer *Southwestern*, I am enabled to give you some account of the fight.
>
> Sunday night, shortly after dark, the boat loaded at a wood pile about a mile above Colfax, Grant parish, and a young fellow, armed to the teeth and very much excited, came aboard and requested the captain to land at Colfax and take some wounded white men to Alexandria, about 25 miles further down the river.
>
> On arriving at Colfax, we found about a hundred armed men on the bank, and most of the passengers, myself among the number, went ashore to view the "battle ground," for our young friend, who came aboard at the wood pile, informed us "that if we wanted to see dead niggers, here was a chance, for there were a hundred or so scattered over the village and the adjacent fields," and he kindly offered to guide us to the scene of action.
>
> Almost as soon as we got to the top of the landing, sure enough, we began to stumble on them, most of them lying on their faces, and, as I could see by the dim light of the lanterns, riddled with bullets.
>
> One poor wretch, a stalwart looking fellow, had been in the burning courthouse, and as he ran out with his clothes on fire, had been shot. His clothes to his waist were all burnt off, and he was literally broiled.
>
> We came upon bodies every few steps, but the sight of this fellow, who was burned, added to the horrible smell of burning human flesh—the remains of those who were shot in the courthouse, which was still on fire—sickened most of us and caused a general cry of "Let's go back."

6. An army investigation concluded that "at least" 105 blacks and 3 whites had been killed at Colfax (*House Executive Documents*, 44th Cong., 2nd Sess., No. 30, pp. 436–38).

7. April 16, 1873.

I counted eighteen of the misguided darkies, and was informed that they were not one-fourth of the number killed; that they were scattered here and there in the fields around the town, besides several in and around the burning courthouse. This, however, was probably an exaggeration.

To show how terribly incensed the people were against the negroes, I relate the following incidents:

We came across one negro whose clothes were smoking, and who had probably been in the fire. Some of our party remarked that he was alive. Instantly one of our guides whipped out a six-shooter, saying "I'll finish the black dog." Of course we remonstrated, and he put away his weapon. Some one stooped down and turned the negro over. He was stiff and cold.

A few minutes afterward we came on a big black fellow, who was reclining on his elbow, and, to all appearances, alive. The man with the six-shooter hit him a fierce kick with his boot, and then stooped down and examined him, saying: "Oh, he's dead as h——l." It was so; the darkey died that way—in a reclining position.

When we came back near the landing the boat's crew were carrying aboard the two wounded white men, a Mr. Hadnot and another whose name I did not learn.

In a store-house near the landing were some twenty or thirty negro prisoners, all huddled together in a corner, with a strong guard over them. I asked one of the guards if I could have some talk with the negroes, but was rather roughly refused.

I do not think any attempt was ever made to show the fact that the largest portion of these people were shot after they had surrendered and been disarmed. I heard rumors of a disturbance at Colfax but nothing definite or even alarming until after their bloody task had been completed. I was then informed by a committee of Democrats of what had taken place, the number of killed and wounded given as somewhere in the hundreds, and told that the desperadoes were on their way up to Coushatta to clean out the Republican officers of Red River Parish. They said that they had nothing against me or my family, and if we kept indoors, none of us would be harmed; only a few troublesome "niggers" would be killed and that would be the end of it. I knew that if the killing commenced our families would suffer in case we were defeated. I told the committee that I would allow no one to be killed in the

parish of Red River and that they could send word to their desperadoes that every colored man, with his gun under my command,
would be ready to meet them before they could reach Coushatta;
that there would be no surrender as at Colfax; and I believed if it
commenced, I could make the Red River valley a desert before the
affair would be over.

The committee withdrew to the hall where the white leaders of
the parish were assembled. They soon returned and asked me how
the difficulty could be avoided and their families and property
saved. I informed them that by placing the white men of the parish under my command, I would undertake to protect all families
and property. They promptly said we place our men under your
command and our women and children under your protection. I
immediately sent two couriers upon each road going south
towards Colfax to inform the people that should any attempt be
made to invade the parish of Red River by the Colfax mob, they
would meet a united people who would tolerate not the slightest
violence to any person, white or black, or however rich or poor he
might be. I had no confidence of being able to use the white men
of the parish and directed them to stay at home with their families. Couriers were sent in all directions to the colored men, directing them to stay at home but to have their horses or riding
mules close at hand, guns ready, and be fully prepared to meet at
Coushatta at the earliest notice.

The white Republican leaders, with horses and arms, were to
remain at Coushatta. In a few hours the parish was thoroughly
alarmed, and the chivalry, feeling confident that they would have
something to do besides shooting unarmed negroes, abandoned
the project.

I had kept the dangers from my family but went home to make
some arrangements which I thought might be necessary, and although apparently calm, my mother insisted that I looked ten
years older than when I left the house in the morning. I found it
quite a serious thing to decide whether there should be war or not
when my mother, wife, and sisters were to be involved in its
horrors.

A few days after the Colfax massacre I was talking with a native
Union white man about the effect of these murders upon the public mind of the North. He seemed to think it would not be great
because only two white men had been killed; and in answer to my

direct question, he said that the killing of ten negroes would not affect public opinion in the North[8] more than the killing of one ordinary white man.

During my residence in the South I had been a close observer of their business customs and methods, had learned their improvidence and wastefulness when they had plenty and their willingness to contract for any price when they were in want. I had noticed that every year corn was purchasable at a low price before Christmas, while after Christmas it was always salable at a high price. In 1873 the corn crop around Starlight was more than abundant, [but] in the hill districts (occupied by poor whites), the crop was comparatively short.

I determined to take advantage of the Southern characteristic of carelessness for the future and gave out word that I would give fifty cents a bushel for all corn delivered at Starlight. I was just beginning to fear that I would not be able to pay for all that was delivered when I learned that the merchants had decided to change their custom and give no credit for 1874. I was at New Orleans attending the session of the Senate and immediately took steps to borrow money and continue, through my agent at Starlight, to purchase the corn.

The spring was well advanced; hill farmers were getting out of corn and applying to the merchants for assistance. This was refused, and an abandonment of their growing crop, with starvation for the next year, was staring them in the face. They turned to me as the only man in the country who could help them. I instructed my agent to give each man but one load of corn, to take no mortgage or any other security for it, charge it to the receiver, and leave it to his honor about the payment. This was an unheard of procedure to them and resulted in such a complete capture of the affections of the people that they declared themselves supporters of mine under all circumstances, not as Democrats or Republicans, but as Twitchellites. I adopted this liberal method of dealing with them, not for political purposes, but because, from my study of Southern character, I had discovered that they would readily pay a debt of honor and let the secured debt go unpaid.

8. The original manuscript has *South* here instead of *North.* This makes no sense in view of the *North* in the first sentence of the paragraph.

18

The White League Revolt, 1874

That winter, as chairman of the finance committee of the Senate, I had the credit of originating the finance bill, by which the state debt was consolidated and scaled down to $15,000,000. For this and other measures I was accorded a position in the affairs of the state so high that the Democrats in my district abandoned the idea of attempting to defeat me in the coming election.

Just before I reached home flushed with success, my wife, Adele, died at Starlight. This so discouraged me that I decided at once to withdraw from public life.

The first time I visited Coushatta, a public reception was given me by the white people, nearly all Democrats, and immediately after, a large public meeting three-fourths of whom were Democrats, was held; and without a dissenting voice, my legislative career for the four years was endorsed. To all appearances there was no man in north Louisiana who stood higher in the regards of the people of all political parties and races; all prejudice arising from politics and service in the Northern army had disappeared. Socially, none seemed so assiduously courted and sought after. I determined to get out of public life, for which I had no taste, and engage with others in some large business enterprises in the country. Calling together the leading Republicans of the district, I proposed to step entirely out of public life and, as a reward to the party which had served me so well, promised to pay their expenses for the next campaign, not to exceed $4,000. While this proposition was being considered, I took charge of my business at Starlight.

In a few weeks the party leaders came to me saying that they could not accept my proposition to retire from the leadership of the party. First, there was no one upon whom they could unite to take my place; and second, there were rumors that the Colfax system was to be followed up, and no one would take the dangerous position of leader. I did not feel that it was right for me to abandon them so long as they were in danger, and accepted the unanimous renomination for state senator. With this nomination as an evidence of my absolute leadership, I met propositions from the Democratic leaders for the nomination of a Union[1] ticket. As a matter of course, the first question of dispute was the relative strength of the two parties among the white people. It was finally decided to call two meetings of the white people on the 4th of July, the one [of] supporters of the Democratic party, and the other of my supporters. The meetings were held, and to the surprise of the opposition, mine was the largest.[2]

The next day I met a lawyer, one of the extreme [Democratic] leaders. After his prudence had been somewhat overcome by the liquid encouragement which he had taken to drown the discouragement of the previous day, he said, "We are not going to compromise but are going to take the offices and the government." In answer to my question he replied, "We have no complaint to make against the way you have run the government in this parish, but you have had it long enough and we are going to take it. We are going to band the white people together, force the white leaders of the Republican party in with us, run them out of the country, or kill them; the negroes will give us no trouble without their white leaders."[3]

1. This probably refers to a united or fusion ticket.
2. The distinction between the White League and the Democratic party was a fine one, because White Leaguers were invariably Democrats. Still, in 1875 Twitchell testified that the July 4 meeting was the first rally of the White League in Red River Parish, and contrary to his contention here, he said that it attracted ninety whites, thirty more than the Republican meeting on Black Lake (*House Reports*, 43rd Cong., 2nd Sess., No. 261, Pt. 3, pp. 386, 394).
3. Twitchell is again confusingly brief about the background of important events. Briefly summarized: the disputed-election crisis of 1872–1873 had both frustrated and emboldened the enemies of Reconstruction in the state. Believing the Radicals had usurped the will of the people, whites felt boundless vexation. On the other hand, the failure of the state and federal governments to react forcefully to the Colfax massacre made direct violence against the Republican government seem increasingly attractive. In March and April, 1874, the White League was born. Bolder even than the Klan and the Knights of the White Camellia, this new terrorist society spread rapidly across the state. In July and August it forced Republican officials in Natchitoches, Red River, and other parishes to re-

Immediately after this the country was full of rumors of mismanagement, embezzlement, and misappropriation of public moneys by Republican officials. The stories were so extravagant that I at first gave but little attention to them, as they seemed to occasion nothing but ridicule. As an illustration, the school board of the parish was charged with embezzling a larger amount of money than had ever passed through its hands. In Red River Parish the source of the stories was a person of doubtful sex, more doubtful sanity, but of unquestionable dishonesty, by the name of Yates.[4]

The [Republican] state convention was called to meet in New Orleans [in August], and as usual I was one of the delegates. Just before I left for the city, a prominent leader of the Republican party, a brave ex-Confederate officer of undoubted ability, learned from his social connections the complete plan of the Democratic party, both as to their movements and the time they were to take place. He said that in a few days the Democrats would take the government of the parish of Natchitoches by force. This would be followed by the seizure of the government of the parish of Red River, and in order to get rid of the Republican leaders, assassination would be resorted to if necessary. He then said that our only chance was to organize a society of a few chosen men and meet them with assassination. This I refused to do. He then remarked that I had better go on to the city and that he was going to take a trip out of the parish. He then called my attention to the stories [of Republican corruption] which had been circulated throughout the country, and it seemed evident to him that I did not understand their object. He said they were for the purpose of affecting public opinion abroad and preparing the way for the assassination and driving out of the Republican leaders. He explained to me what I had not noticed before: that the charges were all made so indefinitely as to persons that when the pressure came, those of the Republicans who went in with the Democratic party would

---

sign their posts and perpetrated the Coushatta massacre. On September 14 the White League in New Orleans—thousands strong and organized into military companies—crushed Governor Kellogg's black militia and the Metropolitan Police in the Battle of Canal Street (renamed the Battle of Liberty Place after Reconstruction). For three days the White League ruled the Crescent City until federal intervention restored the Kellogg government.

4. John T. Yates, former sheriff of Red River Parish.

be claimed as the honest white Republicans, while those who had to be run out or killed would be the rogues.

A few days after my friend warned me to go to the city, I left for the New Orleans convention. As the boat stopped at Campti, a friend came on board and informed me that the mob had that day seized the parish government of Natchitoches. I at first decided to get off the boat and go back to Coushatta by land; but while hesitating on account of there being no conveyance, the boat shoved off, and I was preserved from being included in the first crowd of martyrs.

I had been in New Orleans but a short time before I became convinced, in common with many leading Republicans, that nothing but the presence of United States troops could prevent the Democratic mob from seizing all government in Louisiana which did not recognize the White League as the source and support of its power.

Just after the convention I received letters from my brother, sisters, and Sheriff Edgerton,[5] in which I was informed that an alarming state of affairs existed in Red River Parish. The parish officers had been waited upon by a committee and informed that they must resign or they would be killed. The sheriff asked me what course they should pursue. At the same time he urged me to stay in the city until I could come up with troops, saying that he did not believe anything but the presence of United States troops could prevent bloodshed [and] that in his opinion they were delaying then only for my appearance, so that all of the Republican leaders of that district would be in their power. I at once advised them to resign if that was necessary to prevent bloodshed. Then, in cooperation with the governor and the United States marshal, every possible effort was made to get United States troops sent to Coushatta.

General Emory[6] had been frightened by the White League emissaries into the positive belief that New Orleans was in an epidemic of yellow fever; and he consequently moved all of his troops out of the state, thus placing them beyond the control of the United States marshal of Louisiana, while he, with what seemed to be the most foolish simplicity, did not think anybody was going to be killed, or at least he so acted.

5. Frank S. Edgerton, another Vermont carpetbagger and Union veteran.
6. Major General William H. Emory, commander of the Department of the Gulf.

Without avail we worked until Saturday the 29th of August, when discouraged and worn out, I went over to Pass Christian to spend Sunday with my friend Dewees. For two weeks all communications with our friends and relatives in Coushatta had ceased.

Early Monday morning, August 31st, we received a telegram from my lawyer in Minden saying that Homer J. Twitchell, Robert A. Dewees, F. W. Howell, Clark Holland, Monroe C. Willis, and Sheriff Edgerton had been murdered. This left the parish of Red River without officers [and] robbed Dewees and myself of our only brothers and me of two brothers-in-law, making four widows and three orphans.

We immediately took the train for New Orleans. The governor[7] offered a reward of $5,000 each for the apprehension of the murderers and sent the following telegrams:

New Orleans, La., August 31, 1874
(Via Long Branch, September 1)

To U.S. Attorney General George H. Williams, Washington, D.C.

The statement telegraphed you last night, regarding the outrage at Red River Parish, has been fully confirmed. Further information has just been received that the parish officers and others who surrendered to the White League were being taken to Shreveport by a number of white men. *En route* they were all shot in cold blood. . . . There were six white republicans, all but two northern men, and several colored, murdered in this affair. Red River Parish is near the Texas line, and is among the strongest republican parishes in the State. Predatory bands of armed men are scouring several of the republican parishes in that portion of the State, driving out republicans and intimidating colored men. Registration commenced to-day, and an openly avowed policy of exterminating republicans.

William P. Kellogg.

New Orleans, La., September 1, 1874

To U.S. Attorney General George H. Williams, Washington, D.C.

Sir: We respectfully refer you to the telegram sent to the Washing-

7. Republican governor William Pitt Kellogg and Twitchell developed a close, working relationship that lasted long after Reconstruction was over and both men had left Louisiana. It is pertinent to add that the governor was also a native of Vermont.

ton *National Republican*, giving a detailed account of the outrages recently perpetrated in Coushatta, La., and will state that some of the members of our families were the victims, and that as the State authorities can render no protection for life or property, and further, that as we are citizens of that parish, where our families, houses, and crops are without protection, we implore immediate protection from the United States authorities, and that a company of United States troops be sent to Coushatta at once.

M. H. Twitchell

E. W. Dewees

A. O. P. Pickens

New Orleans, La., September 10, 1874

To U.S. Attorney General George H. Williams, Washington, D.C.

Courier just arrived reports the reign of terror unabated at Coushatta; murders going on daily. A military camp of White Leaguers established in the town, which is being supplied with provisions. We respectfully represent that unless United States troops are sent and retained there, it will be impossible to stop the murder and secure the testimony to prosecute the murderers. Refer to Senator West.

M. H. Twitchell,
State Senator

E. W. Dewees,
Representative, Red River Parish.[8]

I learned from Henry A. Scott and the widows of the murdered men, with other sources of information readily at my disposal, that soon after I left Coushatta for the city, there were continual secret meetings of the white men in the parish, which first resulted in a demand upon the Republican officials to resign their offices. No reason was given for this demand beyond the statement that the white Democrats were going to govern the state without the interference of the negroes or the Republicans.

About the middle of August a party of white men, at night, attacked a negro family, and one of their number was shot and wounded by the negro from his house. The negro was at once killed; but the grave offence of having defended himself in his

---

8. *Senate Executive Documents*, 43rd Cong., 2nd Sess., No. 13, pp. 11–12.

house from his midnight assassins, who chanced to be white, was too serious a matter to be atoned for by the death of one negro.

The secret government, which was already established, sent their couriers into the white settlements with the alarming story that "the negroes on the Red River were rising and killing the white women and children." Great stress was laid upon the supposed dangers to the white women. In a few hours the town was filled with armed white men, and in charge of the new Confederate military government [was] T. W. Abney,[9] captain commanding. All the roads leading into the town were picketed, and a perfect semblance of a "town in siege" was established.

The Republican officers rode to different points in the parish where there were rumors of the negroes rising. In each and every case they found not the slightest shadow had existed for the rumor. In time they became disgusted and informed the Democrats that there was no truth in their story, and all that was wanted to stop the excitement was for the armed men in town to go home about their business.

That night two young men, Dickenson and Pickens, rode out on the Springville road to their picket post. They halted a man in a cotton field, and he not obeying their summons, they fired upon him. The man returned the fire, slightly wounding young Dickenson in the arm.

The next morning different houses were suddenly surrounded by armed military organizations, and Homer J. Twitchell, Clark Holland, F. W. Howell, Frank S. Edgerton, Monroe C. Willis, Robert A. Dewees, and the deputy sheriff, Gilbert Coan,[10] were arrested and put under guard in an unoccupied store. The reasons given for their arrest were that it was necessary to allay the excitement or that it was for their own safety. In no instance were any of them charged with anything wrong. Their actual offence was that they had been so active in going to places of reported [negro] risings and then mingled so freely with the people, assuring them that there was no danger, that it was beginning to dawn upon the minds of the "Woolhats" that they had been unnecessarily called from their work to quell a disturbance which existed only in the minds of the Democratic leaders and their dupes; and

9. Abney was a prominent Coushatta merchant.
10. Why Gilbert Coan was not among those murdered is not known.

it became essential to do something as an excuse for having called so many armed men into town.

At the time these arrests were made, others were ordered in numbers sufficient to keep all the different [White League] companies at work. Two colored men were arrested and hung on a tree just at the edge of the town, serving as amusement for the chivalry and an excuse for keeping together their military force. The reason given for hanging the negroes was for returning young Dickenson's shot and in fact proving a better marksman than he. Only one shot was fired at Dickenson, but as he and Pickens were of the chivalry and loaded down with arms, it was not proper that they should have been so frightened and run back to town by only one of the inferior race; so a second negro must be taken and hanged.

Another party went to the lower end of the parish and arrested Levi Allen. Allen was an intelligent colored man, a leader among his people, honest, industrious, and of great physical strength. He was guilty of having a few weeks before caught the bridle of the horse of a drunken gambler (one of the chivalry) who was attempting to ride him down in the streets of Coushatta.[11]

Allen was at work in the fields [and] made no resistance to the demand that he should go to Coushatta and be examined for his complicity with the riots. As no riots had occurred, he felt, I presume, that nothing could be brought against him and that there was no danger in his going to Coushatta. In passing through the woods he was barbarously wounded, rendering him helpless, and then thrown upon a pile of brush to which fire was set that his dying agonies might be intensified. The chivalry then went on to Coushatta and reported that Allen had escaped in the woods; to their comrades in town they explained with great self-satisfaction how he had escaped.

The parish judge and the postmaster they were unable to find. The judge, a brave ex-Confederate officer, was warned in time and left. The postmaster concealed himself in a dry well, within a few feet of the tree where the colored men were hanged, and baffled all attempts to discover him. My brother-in-law George A. King and John Miller, a visitor from Newfane, Vermont, were at King's

11. In 1875 Twitchell testified that the encounter between Allen and the gambler had occurred two years, not a few weeks, before Allen's arrest (*House Reports*, 43rd Cong., 2nd Sess., No. 261, Pt. 3, p. 389).

plantation eight miles from town, and escaped arrest by hiding in the woods.

Henry A. Scott, formerly of the 11th Vermont Regiment, not an officeholder or citizen of Louisiana, was building a house at Coushatta. He naturally associated with his old friends and army comrades of the Northern element; this made him a suspicious character, and he was arrested with the others. He was a Baptist deacon from Townshend, Vermont, where he was active in church and sabbath-school work, as well as a prominent Mason. For a short time he endeavoured to be active in the establishment of a sabbath school at Coushatta. In some manner he was soon informed that his ideas and system were not in accord with the view of the white people of that locality, and consequently his prominence as a sabbath-school worker disappeared.

His case was considered by the military council, which was greatly relieved when he made application to T. W. Abney to be released from arrest as a Master Mason. Abney caused him to be brought out to his house and then to his barn, promising to keep him concealed, and finally put him out of the town. Scott's experience for the preceding few weeks had materially lessened his confidence in Southern honor and promises. He escaped through the pickets at night with one of my horses, assumed a name and character, and with a good deal of address and remarkable good luck made a successful trip to Colfax (75 miles), the nearest station of the United States troops, representing himself to the white people as a courier from Captain Abney at Coushatta.

After the hanging of the negroes—their last amusement—there had been nothing more exciting than opening letters that came by mail addressed to Republicans or examining stores and houses of prominent Republicans, as they claimed, for arms. Some companies coming from a distance felt that they had done nothing, and clamoured for the murder of the men under arrest.

This was not desired by Abney and his council. They felt that such an outrage would receive at least a certain notice and would give the resident leaders more trouble than was desirable. It was finally decided that they should be put under guard and sent out of the parish before they were harmed. I have no doubt but that in this last movement there was much deceit used among the Democratic leaders. Some desired and expected that the prisoners should be allowed to safely reach Northern territory. I think the prisoners believed that the promise of their being conducted to a place of safety was to be carried out, although the earnest appeal of my brother that they should be allowed their arms as well as their own horses seemed to indicate that he had fears of treachery.

The women and children of the prisoners left at Coushatta had no doubt of the good faith of the Democrats. Some influence that was strong enough to let my brother go to the courthouse under guard and open the safe, directed the prisoners to take all their valuables with them that they could carry, the murderers thereby making their victims pay for their own murder, as horses, watches, rings, money, and everything of value, even some of their clothing, was [later] divided among the murderers. That this was allowed by the anti-murder party shows that they were too weak to interfere or were indifferent to the safety of the prisoners.

After two hours' delay, the prisoners were started up the river to Shreveport, where they were expecting to take the cars for the North. They rode rapidly until just beyond the parish line, where the guards insisted upon a halt for rest and refreshment. Suddenly an armed crowd with Dick Coleman,[12] a noted desperado, at their head came up. Dewees first observing the danger cried, "Mount and ride for your lives." They were soon on their horses but too late to be of any avail. Dewees was shot from his horse before he was hardly seated in the saddle. My brother was shot in the face and attempted to seize a gun from one of the guards, crying out, "Give me a gun, I don't want to die like a dog." Edgerton, throwing himself flat upon his horse, escaped the first volley and made considerable distance before he was finally shot from his horse, answering back to their calls of surrender that he would die first. Holland, Willis, and Howell obeyed the first call to surrender.

The murderers, with the last three, crossed the river to Ward's store, Bossier Parish. Here a number of hours was spent in consultation about what was best to do with the prisoners. A planter by the name of Stringfellow offered $1,000 apiece to save the lives of the three prisoners, but this could not be paid down, and finally Dick Coleman's counsel prevailed that it was best to murder the prisoners, take their horses and valuables, and remove important witnesses of the previous murders. Howell and Willis were

12. As far as is known, no relation to Adele Coleman's family.

brought out in front of the store and, after the manner of a military execution, were coolly shot down. Holland for some reason was offered an opportunity to leave the store and run down the cotton rows towards the swamps, holding out to him the chance that he might escape. He seemed to understand that the savages only wanted the amusement of hunting and shooting, and replied, "No, you have murdered my friends, now you may kill me," and he stepped forward to the bodies of Willis and Howell and received the murderous volley, asking of his pretended friends only one favor, which was that his wife and little boy might be allowed to escape North unharmed.

I have no doubt but that the fate of the prisoners was fully decided and known by the active leaders before they left Coushatta, although I presume there were many [who] hoped that in some way they might escape, and some who thought they were to be allowed to safely leave the country.

A conspiracy to murder was commenced at Coushatta, parish of Red River. The crime was partially committed in the parish of Caddo and the other part in the parish of Bossier. A crime [was] commenced in the jurisdiction of one court and completed within the jurisdiction of two other courts, placing as many difficulties as they conveniently could in the way of prosecution. The apologies for this crime attach much importance to the fact that the prisoners were allowed to choose their own route and in part their own guard. It must be remembered that all active friends of the prisoners were run out of the country or [were] in hiding to escape arrest, and the guard was selected from the former Democratic social friends of the prisoners, who were the first under arms at Coushatta to assist in their arrest and retention.

As a matter of fact these friendly guards, upon one excuse and another, had all fallen out and were not up with the prisoners at the time of the murder. If there had been any strong influence in favor of saving their lives, they would have been given their arms, and the story of the Coushatta massacre would read wonderfully unlike the present history of that event. The whole story is for the chivalry one of treachery, cowardice, and dishonor.

The prisoners submitted to arrest upon the assurance of the Democratic leaders that it would allay the excitement, prevent the murder of negroes, and protect from harm the women and children belonging to them. They were kept disarmed so that they could offer no dangerous resistance to their own murder and robbery, to the brave and honorable chivalry that, according to their own statement, never strikes a fallen foe.

As a matter of fact the so-called Southern chivalry is a remnant of the dark ages which they copy, and although they have some desirable qualities, they also have many of the savage and barbarous characteristics of the lower civilization to which they belong.

During the political and factional fights in New Orleans, I had become acquainted with many of the gang leaders of roughs which infest the city and are always for sale to the highest bidder. From them I learned that there was no question but that the state government would be assailed soon. I visited the United States marshal's office (our headquarters) and urged immediate preparation to meet the emergency. I could not, either with honor or safety, give the source of the information or impress others with the full gravity of the situation; they seemed to expect a number of weeks' delay. Disgusted with their apathy, Dewees and I went over to his house at Pass Christian to await the appearance of a danger sufficiently vivid for our friends to see it.

On the 14th of September it came with such irresistible force as to overturn the state government and confine all legal authority in the state to the Custom House, where the governor and all prominent Republicans were compelled to take refuge to save their lives. The next day, fearing that all property belonging to prominent Republicans would be seized, I decided to go to New Orleans, visit the Louisiana Safe Deposit Company, and remove some securities of mine and my friend Dewees to the Custom House.

I relied upon my thorough acquaintance with the city and what would be considered my foolhardiness and the consequent surprise which the White League police would feel at seeing me on the street, taken in connection with my rapid movements, for the success of my undertaking. I stepped off the cars at the Canal Street station, walked rapidly to the savings bank and from there to the Custom House. After some delay the doors were opened for my admission and I deposited the securities in the Custom House safe. I do not know who was the most surprised, my enemies on the street as I passed them at a rapid walk, or my friends in the Custom House at my appearance there.

Just before the train went back to Pass Christian again, to the surprise of everybody I left the Custom House, walked through the city down to the Claiborne Street station, and took the train, leaving the guard who had been placed at the Canal Street station for my arrest to report that I was still in the city. My friend at the Pass could hardly believe that I had so quickly and safely accomplished our purpose.

The overturning of the state government on the 14th of September, by the defeat of the militia in a pitched battle with the reorganized Confederacy, convinced the Federal authorities that it was time for the use of United States troops. The state government was at once reinstated in New Orleans and in some other portions of the state. In the parish of Red River, the sheriff, tax collector, prosecuting attorney, supervisor of registration, and one justice of the peace had been murdered; the other officers were driven from the parish.

The allies of the Confederacy in the Northern states, with their characteristic cowardice, urged their Southern friends to stop armed resistance and turn their attention to carrying the state for the Democrats in November. It was believed that by the murder of so many leading Republicans in the state, the negroes would be sufficiently intimidated to dispose of the Louisiana Republican majority of 10,000.

On or about the 1st of October, I started up to Coushatta with two companies of United States troops and commissions for parish officers, to reestablish the parish government. On the way up the river, the white people greeted me with sullen frowns, and the colored with cheers, waving of hats and handkerchiefs, showing every possible evidence of joy. Captain Jack (Dick Coleman) kept some of his roughs in Coushatta the night before we arrived, to attack the boat; but wisely for him, he gave up the idea, and we landed without any demonstration being made.

I found the parish under semimilitary government, Captain T. W. Abney commanding, with whom I immediately entered into the following agreement, as a temporary measure until the state authority and parish government was finally established:

CITIZEN CONFERENCE COMMITTEE
T. W. Abney, President. Julius Lisso, Secretary.
W. S. Williams, F. Roubieu, J. W. Sandiford, A. F. Stephinson,
C. D. Bullock, B. W. Marston, D. I. Dupree, W. A. Perry
Jno. E. Murph, B. S. Lee
Col. J. M. Sandidge, of New Orleans, was invited to participate.

Coushatta, La., Oct. 6, 1874

In accord with that spirit of conciliation and justice which seems to have prevailed in effecting an arrangement, in New Orleans, between Gov. Kellogg and his friends and Gov. McEnery and his friends and those opposed to the Kellogg administration, for conducting all matters connected with the approaching election, and a general pacification of the country: It is agreed between M. H. Twitchell representing the Kellogg administration, in this parish, and as acting United States Commissioner, sent here to enquire into the recent Coushatta troubles, and as president of the police jury on the one part, and the committee of citizens, appointed for that purpose at a public meeting of the citizens of the parish held at the Court-house Monday the 5th of October 1874 on the other part—

That to secure a full and fair expression of the will of the people at the November election, a just administration of the affairs of the parish; and quieting the mind of the people, so greatly excited by recent disturbances in this and other parishes of the state—
1. The officers of the parish which have been, or may hereafter be filled by Executive appointment, shall be of resident citizens of this parish, including Supervisor of Registration, and the two clerks to act under him.
2. The registration and Election shall be conducted in strict accordance with the instructions of the joint commission appointed to supervise the same in New Orleans and a joint committee similar to that in New Orleans, shall be selected to supervise the registration and election in Red River parish, and the commissioners of election; the polling precincts, and all other matters connected with the election shall be left to said committee, whose advice shall control any action of the Police Jury and all other officers, having any connection with the election, in relation thereto.
[3.] M. H. Twitchell, for himself, and in his capacity of United States Commissioner, declares that it is not his purpose to disquiet the minds of the public and that he will have no citizen arrested on

account of the recent disturbances in this parish, except it be those engaged in the murder of F. S. Edgerton and others on or about the 30th of August last and that to avoid unnecessary hardships and delays, and to afford the readiest possible means of showing their innocence, any party arrested on charge of participating in said killing, shall have the right to be heard immediately before the commissioner at Coushatta with witness[es] and shall be discharged on reasonable proof of innocence. And in default of such showing may be held to answer under bond or otherwise.

Should any citizen be charged or suspected with being of the party mentioned above, voluntarily appear before the acting Commissioner, demanding an inquiry as to such charge, such person shall be allowed to return to his home without molestation, or *surveillance*, whatever may be the evidence for or against him, free from further inquiry, should his proof of innocence be satisfactory; and subject to arrest afterwards, if deemed necessary to meet the demands of the law. It being the object of this clause of the agreement to obviate the arrest of any citizen who might be deemed liable to be arrested as a co-conspirator in consequence of any action taken by him in the recent Coushatta troubles, and to mean that only such as are charged with the actual perpetration of any homicide should be arrested and held to trial.

That we earnestly desire and invoke an inquiry into all matters connected with the recent occurrences in the parish of Red River.
4. The committee representing the Conservative People's party pledge themselves, as far as in their power, to cause all violence and intimidation, if any exists, to cease throughout the parish, and to assist the constituted authorities in maintaining peace, and insuring a strictly fair and impartial registration and election; also, to discountenance all acts of personal violence and all improper influences to control the will of the electors; and to render assistance and to use every effort to subject to the penalties of the law all persons who may commit acts of violence or intimidation, or conspire to do the same.
5. It is agreed that if the Republican party, retain the Supervisor of Registration, the People's party shall have the choice of the two clerks thereof.

The agreement is subject to ratification by the people at a mass meeting to be held at Coushatta on Thursday October 8th 1874.
   (Signed)

A. F. Stephens [*sic*]   W. S. Williams
C. D. Bullock   F. Roubieu
D. I. Dupree   B. W. Marston
B. S. Lee   W. A. Perry
J. W. Sandiford   Jno. E. Murhh [*sic*]
T. W. Abney   M. H. Twitchell
                   Julius Lisso, Secretary [13]

In my effectual attempts to [re]establish the parish government, I discovered that the leaders of the society who had set the ball of revolution rolling doubted their power to stop it. The irresponsible elements of society with nothing to lose by a state of anarchy, who were petted by the leaders while doing their bidding, objected to dropping back into the places of nonentity from which they had been so recently raised.

After many consultations they finally informed me that the mob element was determined to kill me as soon as the boat returned from Shreveport and took back one company of United States troops. As the boat came in sight, a committee urged me to return with the troops. Almost immediately thereafter another committee urged me to make the appointment of parish officers so that an election might be held.

I walked onto the boat through the mob, who were only waiting for it to shove off before they seized me, and then informed the committee that I had decided to return to New Orleans and they must learn to control the mob before the day of election if they had an election at all. Had they known what my decision was to have been before I reached the boat, I should never have reached it, as I well knew. There was a few minutes of stir and excitement on the bank, but evident preparation by the troops caused them to recognize that they had been beaten and that their victim had escaped again.

My return to New Orleans, taken in connection with the refusal of the governor to give the government of those parishes to the Democratic committee, was an annoying event to the revolutionary leaders. The four parishes of my senatorial district had

13. The names on this document comprise a who's who of the Coushatta business community. Marshall Harvey Twitchell Scrapbook (Microfilm copy in Marshall Harvey Twitchell Papers, Prescott Memorial Library, Louisiana Tech University, Ruston).

been thoroughly revolutionized by the murder of Republicans, to such an extent that it was embarrassing their Democratic allies in the North much more than had been anticipated. And for them to lose in the coming election the vote which they had converted so effectually with their shotguns and at such an expense in Northern sentiment was something which they could not endure.

The leaders in New Orleans quickly made arrangements by which they could guarantee the safety of Republican supervisors of registration so that a registration and election might take place. They calculated very properly that they could seize what did not suit them after the election had taken place.

19

Election of 1874

I returned to Coushatta just in time to meet a detachment of the 7th United States Cavalry which had arrested a number of the prominent leaders of the Coushatta Massacre. This action seemed to satisfy the people that the Federal authorities did not approve of their assassinations and even had power to arrest their leaders. Before this feeling had worn off, they were made acquainted with the policy of their leaders that the country must be quiet enough to have an election. During registration there was no more quiet section than the Red River parishes, a peace which I knew would continue until the day of the election.

The parishes of Sabine and De Soto, in which there were no U.S. troops, I knew would not be allowed to return Republican majorities even if Republicans were allowed to vote; consequently, we made the best possible arrangements to secure evidence of intimidation and fraud, collecting through my agents some of the posters, as evidence of their intention, like the following:

MASS MEETING of the CITIZENS OF DE SOTO PARISH,
Oct. 26, 1874

At a meeting held this day at the hall of Ward No. 2, the following resolutions were unanimously adopted:

Resolved, That we, the citizens of Ward No. 2, in convention assembled, do most solemnly pledge ourselves to refuse to employ, rent land to, or in any manner whatever, give aid or comfort to any man who votes the radical ticket at the coming election. This is not, however, to affect directly or indirectly, any existing contract.[1]

1. Broadside, in Marshall Harvey Twitchell Scrapbook (Microfilm copy in Marshall Harvey Twitchell Papers, Prescott Memorial Library, Louisiana Tech University, Ruston), hereinafter cited as MHT Scrapbook.

In the parish of Red River two polls were established in the town of Coushatta. No attempt was made to disturb them on account of the camp of United States troops just outside of the town. Secret instructions were given to all Republican voters in the parish, who could be reached after dark, to come to Coushatta during the night so that they would be able to avoid pickets which might be placed upon the road to prevent coming after daylight. At the outlying polls I suggested that one of the commissioners should be a colored man.

The election passed off, almost without an exception, as anticipated. Sabine, which in 1870 polled 432 Republican and 347 Democratic votes, returned 762 Democratic and 2 Republican [votes]. In De Soto, the Democrats with shotguns took charge of all the polling places in such direct violation of law and decency that the supervisor, as soon as he had reached a place of safety in New Orleans, refused to make any returns, and the 1870 Republican majority was suppressed. [In] Natchitoches, in which the colored vote is very large, the suppression was much more difficult. They succeeded only in suppressing 932 of the Republican majority, while in Red River Parish they suppressed 257 of the Republican majority.[2]

So far as getting votes into the box were concerned, the local leaders of the Democratic party were well pleased. But by [my] refusing to talk about the election or to recognize my defeat, they were led to study with more thoroughness the position.[3] In Sabine and De Soto they began to fear that they had done too much, while in Red River and Natchitoches the Democratic votes had been polled in boxes, where they had driven away the colored commissioner or had violated the law by appearing at the polls with arms.

A rumor was current the night before the election that some more arrests were to be made on the next day. This perhaps had the effect of causing the Democrats to vote at the outlying polls and afterwards, under whisky influence, to drive away the colored commissioner. Some of the better lawyers, in reading up the law,

2. The figures for Sabine Parish are confirmed in *House Miscellaneous Documents*, 45th Cong., 3rd Sess., No. 31, Pt. 1 (insert contains election returns for entire period). How Twitchell arrived at the number of suppressed votes in Natchitoches and Red River is unclear, but his figures appear to be exaggerated.

3. Twitchell's defeat by J. B. Elam of De Soto Parish was reversed in December by the state returning board.

discovered that there was great danger that those boxes, in which was the bulk of the Democratic votes, could be thrown out; and putting all things together, they made up their minds that they had walked into a trap set for them by the wicked radicals.

I was looked upon as the manager of the [radical] party, and it was decided that I should not be allowed to leave the parish to appear before the returning board[4] in New Orleans. This plan of theirs was fully understood by me and my friends. We knew that all the common routes to New Orleans would be well taken care of. Selecting four fast horses, I had two placed at a friend's ten miles west of Coushatta. Saturday afternoon I called on the doctor, who was in their political councils, for medicine (which I took good care not to take), went to my house, closed the blinds of my room, and prepared to be sick. As soon as it was dark, we left Coushatta for New Orleans by an unusual and circuitous route, which commenced with seventy-five miles on horseback through one of the most sparsely settled districts in north Louisiana. A very rapid ride of ten miles brought us to the house of a trusty friend where two of the best horses in Louisiana were ready for us. In five minutes the saddles were changed and we were again on our way. My companion and guide was an ex-Confederate soldier of notorious bravery and so familiar with the country that we could at any time have left the road and continued our journey in the woods.

About midnight we heard someone cross a bridge behind us; instantly our horses were checked and our revolvers made ready. I proposed that we ride into the woods a few paces and let them pass. My friend replied as he loosened his rein, "That is not necessary; there was only one crossed the bridge, and no one or two men are going to follow us." His better knowledge of the courage of men who did the dirty work of the [Democratic] party served us a good purpose. Just before daylight we reached Black Lake Bayou, which we swam, much to our discomfort, to prevent leaving with the ferryman the knowledge that we had crossed. At ten o'clock we were at the house of my father-in-law's old foreman, where we fed our horses and rested for an hour.

4. The Republicans created the state returning board in the election law of 1870. This potent agency compiled the returns of every election and had the power to discard the votes of any precincts in which, in its judgment, fraud or intimidation occurred. With good reason, it was greatly feared by the Democratic party.

At the rate we were travelling, my guide correctly judged that about dark we would reach Vienna, a small town run by whisky and the White League. My prominence in political life and the souvenir of the Wilderness on my left cheek rendered it almost certain that there would be someone at the hotel who would recognize me. We pushed on through Vienna a couple of miles and stopped at a farmhouse. I never exerted myself more to please, or guarded my Northern peculiarities of speech closer than I did that evening. We went to bed with the satisfaction of having kept the people so thoroughly amused that they had forgotten to ask any questions concerning their guests.

In the morning my friend visited the horses [and] gave the negro who was attending them a quarter with instructions to have them brought to the door by the time we had finished breakfast. We kept out of the way of conversation until breakfast was announced. Just before we had finished our meal and after I had seen our horses pass the window, our host, as was customary, asked our names. I immediately gave my name and address at Coushatta so that the old gentlemen might not have the least doubt who I was. I had seen many surprises in my life but none which exceeded that of old Mr. Kidd and his family. He politely declined pay for our entertainment and with much civility bade us good morning as we walked out to our horses. So well was the idea of my confinement to the house from sickness carried out by my sister Helen that I had reached New Orleans before my absence was discovered.

All general interest in the election was for the members of the legislature, it being the plan of the Democratic leaders to [obtain a majority and] then impeach the Republican state officers and amend the election law which gave the returning board authority to throw out polls for violence and fraud, when everything would be easy for them to accomplish.

They considered it very important that the legislature should be elected with such apparent fairness that public opinion of the North would be satisfied; consequently, it was with the greatest annoyance that they received despatches from their friends in the country of the suppression of the entire Republican vote, when it was only Republican majorities that they had wanted suppressed.

They quickly discovered that their too-zealous partisans had so greatly overdone their work that it would never pass by the returning board even if the willing, blind public opinion of the North was satisfied. But they had gone too far to retreat; at any cost the evidence of fraud and intimidation must be prevented from appearing before the returning board. Witnesses, candidates, and returning board must be intimidated or killed. In the Democratic organ in my district, the following article or instructions appeared.

The True Policy

We want no representative on the returning board; no favors or concessions from Kellogg and Packard. . . .

We know the results of the election in every parish. . . . Therefore we should simply give the members of that board to distinctly understand that, unless they return the elections as they were returned at the polls, they and those they seek to "count in," will pay the forfeit with their lives.

We have no appeals to make to our fellow-citizens of New Orleans; we know that the men of the 14th of September will do their whole duty as freemen, and Louisianians zealous of their liberties. But throughout the country parishes there should be concert of action, and that action should be prompt and emphatic. In every parish where the officers elected by the people may be counted out by the returning board, the people should use hemp or ball on the defeated candidates counted in. To localize the proposition: If Geo. L. Smith is counted in over W. M. Levy, or if Twitchell is counted in over Elam, let Smith and Twitchell be killed; if Johnson and Tyler, in De Soto, are counted in over Scales and Schuler, as the New Orleans *Republican* threatens, or if Keeting, Levisee and Johnson in Caddo are counted in over Vaughan, Horan and Land, then let Johnson, Tyler, Keeting, Levisee and Johnson be killed; and so let every officer, from Congressman down to constable; in every district and parish of the State, be served whom the people have defeated and whom the returning board may "count in."

We cannot afford to be defeated by a ring of political scoundrels after we have triumphed. . . . Human life may be precious; but the lives of all the carpet-baggers and radical politicians in Louisiana, are valueless, compared with the worth of a single principle of justice and liberty.[5]

5. Shreveport (La.) *Times*, November 15, 1874, in MHT Scrapbook.

That the *Republican* had no right to presume that this was an idle threat is shown by the following extract from General Sheridan's report [on the White League].

Telegram. New Orleans, January 10, 1875—11.30 p.m.
To W. W. Belknap, Secretary of War, Washington, D.C.

Since the year 1866 nearly thirty-five hundred persons, a great majority of whom were colored men, have been killed and wounded in this State. In 1868 the official record shows that eighteen hundred and eighty-four were killed and wounded. From 1868 to the present time no official investigation has been made, and the civil authorities, in all but a few cases, have been unable to arrest, convict, and punish perpetrators. Consequently, there are no correct records to be consulted for information. There is ample evidence, however, to show that more than twelve hundred persons have been killed and wounded during this time on account of their political sentiments. Frightful massacres have occurred in the parishes of Bossier, Caddo, Catahoula, Saint Bernard, Saint Landry, Grant, and Orleans. The general character of the massacres in the above-named parishes is so well known that it is unnecessary to describe them.

The isolated cases can best be illustrated by the following instances, which I take from a mass of evidence now lying before me of men killed on account of their political principles: In Natchitoches Parish, the number of isolated cases reported is thirty-three; in the parish of Bienville the number of men killed is thirty; in Red River Parish the isolated cases of men killed is thirty-four; in Winn Parish the number of isolated cases where men were killed is fifteen; in Jackson Parish the number killed is twenty; and in Catahoula Parish the number of isolated cases reported where men were killed is fifty, and most of the country parishes throughout the State will show a corresponding state of affairs. The following statements will illustrate the character and kind of these outrages:

On the 30th of August, 1874, in Red River Parish, six State and parish officers, named Twitchell, Divers [sic], Holland, Howell, Edgerton, and Willis, were taken, together with four negroes, under guard to be carried out of the State, and were deliberately murdered on the 29th of August, 1874 [sic]. The White League tried, sentenced, and hung two negroes on the 28th of August, 1874. Three negroes were shot and killed at Brownsville, just before the arrival of the United States troops in this parish. Two white-leaguers rode up to a negro cabin and called for a drink of water. When the old colored man turned to draw it, they shot him in the back and killed him. The courts were all broken up in this district, and the district judge driven out. . . .

P. H. Sheridan,
Lieutenant-General[6]

By the terrorism of the murders committed they had effectually suppressed thousands of Republican votes and very naturally believed that the candidates and returning board could be similarly influenced. The vote suppressed was from the race rendered timid by the debasing influences of slavery. The class which they now wished to reach was composed of Unionists hardened by three years of persecution for loyalty, the ex-Federal soldier tested upon many a hard-fought field of battle, and with a superior and educated body of colored men, all strengthened and determined from the justice of their cause.

The returning board met under the protection of the United States troops and, with the utmost liberality, accorded to the Democrats all seats in which there was the slightest grounds for belief that they had a majority. Under the law, where proof was furnished, they threw out many of the intimidated districts. This had a very unfair effect against the Republicans in the composition of the legislature, as it was in these districts that vacancies were created in place of Republican members who would have been elected but for the intimidation.[7]

After nearly three months of semi-revolution under the "Wheeler Compromise,"[8] the legislature was organized with a

6. *Congressional Record*, 43rd Cong., 2nd Sess., 421.

7. The returning board's count of the votes, proclaimed December 24, was anything but liberal as far as the Democrats were concerned—it deprived them of a majority in the house of representatives. The Christmastide announcement set the stage for the stormy meeting of the legislature in January, 1875, in which, once again, only the intervention of federal troops stopped a coup against the Kellogg government (Ella Lonn, *Reconstruction in Louisiana After 1868* [New York, 1918], 289–99).

8. More commonly called the Wheeler Adjustment, it was named after Republican Congressman William A. Wheeler of New York. He was a member of the House subcommittee that arbitrated this latest Louisiana election controversy in the winter of 1875. The terms of the adjustment were these: The Democrats agreed to stop trying to overthrow Kellogg's government, and the Republicans accepted Democratic control of the Louisiana lower house. Although formally endorsed by both houses of the legislature in April, the cease fire was stoutly resisted

Republican majority in the Senate and a Democratic majority in the House. After a short session of ten days in which the Wheeler Compromise was legalized and a few acts necessary for carrying on the state government were passed, the legislature adjourned.

This summer [of 1875] I visited the North and purchased the General [Pardon T.] Kimbell place in Newfane, Vermont, where I moved my mother and her three orphan grandsons, fully determined that the Southern chivalry should not have the opportunity of carrying out their threat to murder all the males of the family. When I returned to Coushatta in October, I became fully satisfied, from private sources, that a revolution would be attempted during the coming winter to gain possession of the executive branch of the government.

I reached New Orleans early in November, hurried away by my sisters, who were in constant fear that I would be assassinated. I had hardly become settled when I received a telegram from Starlight informing me that Mrs. Holland (sister Kate) had died from yellow fever on the 14th and was buried at Starlight by the side of her murdered husband.

---

by important segments of both parties and broke down in 1876 (Joe Gray Taylor, *Louisiana Reconstructed, 1863–1877* [Baton Rouge, 1974], 308–309). Congressman Wheeler went on to become vice-president under Hayes.

20

Crisis in the Legislature, 1876

On the first Monday in January, 1876, the legislature met for the memorable session in which the governor was impeached, tried, and acquitted all in one day. My habits of industry and temperance, in connection with the belief that I would not be frightened from doing my duty, together with my good physical endurance, which enabled me to remain in the Senate chamber without rest during the longest session, caused me to be elected chairman of the Republican caucus and manager of my party in the Senate. The session was one long, continuous struggle between the Democratic majority of the House and the Republican majority of the Senate. I consider this the most trying of all my public experience.

Many of the Republicans were discouraged and disgusted by the apparent willingness of the North to allow them—and the right—to be sacrificed that they might get rid of a troublesome object. The Democrats were encouraged by this action and were ready with money and promises to work upon any weak Republican whom they could reach. Many a time in the Republican caucus, to offset these influences, we were compelled to call attention to the many murders of our friends and comrades yet unpunished.

The hardest part of our work was to keep up the courage of weak senators so as to retain our majority in that body. I had served four years in the Senate. The Republican senators were, without exception, men with whom I was well acquainted, knowing all their peculiarities and their weaknesses. In true army style they were divided so that in protracted sessions, where the purpose was to tire us out, I could allow my party to go to their meals by reliefs, taking good care that no two weak ones should go by themselves. No one seemed to think, nor did I, that it was at all necessary for me to leave the chamber for either meals or rest.

I remember one day in which the struggle was so continuous, extending even into the morning hours, my mind was so occupied that I entirely forgot it was necessary for me to eat, and retired without having tasted food since my breakfast. In the morning at the restaurant I remarked that I was not feeling well. The waiter replied, "I noticed that you did not come to your dinner yesterday." It then occurred to me for the first time that I had forgotten to dine the day before. A good breakfast cured my sickness.

The crisis of the winter came when the House passed resolutions impeaching the governor. This movement had been carefully planned and the Democrats believed that success was certain. All bills required for the interest of the state which the two houses could agree upon had been passed. It was decided that immediately after the resolution had passed, the House should adjourn for three days (constitutional limit without consent of the Senate), and during these three days it was expected that the government would be overturned and enough Republican senators disposed of or changed so that when the Senate met for the trial, there would be a majority for his impeachment. Better than any other living man, I knew the danger of exposing the Republican senators to the machinations of the Democrats outside the Senate chamber and unsupported by each other's presence.

The House appointed me manager to appear before the Senate with their articles of impeachment, intending by this course to prevent the Senate from acting upon the articles immediately. On being informed of its action by a friend in the House, I called an executive session and then confidentially informed my Republican colleagues of what had taken place and that we must remain in session until the course which we should pursue had been decided.

Governor Kellogg with fifteen or twenty of the leading Republicans of the state were in a short time together in the lieutenant governor's private room to consult upon the question. The chief justice of the state was somewhat averse to any hasty or unjudicial proceedings, and when I entered the room, it seemed as though, with the single exception of ex-Governor Warmoth, all were in favor of proceeding slowly and with judicial fairness. As soon as it was possible for me to speak, I informed them that with the adjournment of the state Senate all vestige of Republican government in Louisiana would disappear, that I knew a Republican majority in the chamber would not be possible three days later if we adjourned with the governor suspended, that the trial must take place at once, without it was the intention of the party leaders to abandon the contest for Republican government in the state.

Someone remarked that the trial in such haste would be irregular. I replied that if assassination and revolution could be checked and right prevail with a slight judicial irregularity, I thought we had better have the irregularity. My opinion prevailed, and the doors of the Senate were immediately opened and the high court of impeachment formed.

Rules for the government of the court were immediately adopted, the secretary of the Senate instructed to notify the House, and a recess of thirty minutes taken to give the House managers time to appear before the Senate with their articles of impeachment. The time passed, court was opened, and I offered the following order:

> Whereas, The House of Representatives has notified the Senate that it has impeached William P. Kellogg, Governor of the State of Louisiana, of high crimes and misdemeanors; and
>
> Whereas, Said House has acted in said impeachment contrary to law in this, that it has refused to permit said William P. Kellogg, Governor of the State of Louisiana, to appear before the committee appointed to investigate the charges made against him, either in person or by counsel, and has refused to furnished [sic] him with a list of the witnesses relied upon to support said charges; and
>
> Whereas, It is a notorious fact that said impeachment is prompted by partisan and revolutionary purpose; and
>
> Whereas, It was agreed by said House, by act No. 1 of the extra session of 1875, in pursuance of the terms of the agreement known as the Wheeler adjustment, that said William P. Kellogg, Governor of the State of Louisiana, should not be impeached for any acts committed prior to the adoption of said act, and that the House of Representatives would henceforth accord to him full support in the maintenance of the laws and the promotion of the welfare of the people and the State; and
>
> Whereas, This resolution of impeachment is in violation of said agreement; and

Whereas, The acts of the said William P. Kellogg as Governor of the State of Louisiana are fully known to each and every member of this Senate, and known to us not to be criminal or unlawful;

Whereas, The Senate has adopted a notice for the House to appear and make good its charges; and

Whereas, Said House has hurriedly adjourned until next Wednesday, at 10 A.M., knowing that but little more than one day of the session will then remain; and

Whereas, This adjournment is believed to have been taken for the purpose of defeating a full investigation of said charges; and

Whereas, We believe the said William P. Kellogg, Governor of the State of Louisiana, to be innocent of any criminal act or of any high crime or misdemeanor; and

Whereas, The resolution adopted by the House of Representatives recites no specific grounds of impeachment against the said William P. Kellogg; and

Whereas, The House of Representatives has failed to appear and present any specific charges or accusations against the said William P. Kellogg, Governor, notwithstanding said House has had full and sufficient time for said purpose;

It is ordered that [*i.e.*, by] the Senate, sitting as a Court of Impeachment, That the impeachment presented by the House of Representatives be dismissed by reason of the failure of said House to prosecute the same, and that this order have the same force and effect as a judgement of acquittal.[1]

The Democrats, finding that their plan must be changed to meet our unexpected move, hastily appointed a management committee which appeared in the Senate and claimed recognition. It was known to all present that the House had appointed no committee before its adjournment, equally as well known that they had been adjourned for a number of hours, and that legally no committee could have been appointed.

Mr. Wiltz, a member of the House, afterwards lieutenant governor and governor,[2] one of the pretended members of the committee, came into the Senate chamber and in a dictatorial style demanded that he should be heard. He commenced an exciting and revolutionary speech. I called for order and demanded that the

1. *Louisiana Senate Journal*, 1876, pp. 289–95.
2. Louis Alfred Wiltz was speaker of the house in 1875, lieutenant governor from 1877 to 1880 and governor from 1880 to 1881.

gentleman who was disturbing the high court of impeachment of the State of Louisiana be removed that the proceedings of the court might be continued. The chief justice discovered at once that we did not intend to give the House any chance to recover from their mistake of not appointing a committee to prosecute the governor before it adjourned. He directed the sergeant at arms to remove the noisy gentleman who was disturbing the court.

Thus the last move of the Democratic House failed. After many hours of parliamentary struggle, my order was adopted, the governor acquitted, and the high court of impeachment adjourned, *sine die.*

As a member of a high court of impeachment for the first time, acting under rules which I had hardly read, I lacked the confidence in myself which I felt on the floor of the Senate; consequently, it was with a great deal of satisfaction that I read the interview of the Chicago *Tribune* with Governor Kellogg the next summer, of which the following is an extract: " . . . Twitchell was a leader in Louisiana. He was a match for the rebel element in the Legislature. He was successful against eight good lawyers in the impeachment business, and I think he is a man of great ability."[3]

The following is an extract from the Mansfield *Reporter* which seemed to express the opinion of my enemies in regard to my winter's work:

> . . . That the Governor was guilty of some of the charges preferred against him was true, that he was guilty of the whole is a question which can never now be known to the public more than assumptively. If the move was a political one which is maintained by some, the measure of its success is yet to be tested, if it was actuated by stern motives of duty to the State and our people, we cannot see why it might not as well have been done forty days ago. It must have been apparent at that time, that the Republican majority of the Senate, controled as it was by that shrewd, silent, unscrupulous, untiring Machievelli of that body, the suppositious Senator from this district, M. H. Twitchell, would never yield to the demands of the House. It must have been equally as apparent then as afterwards, that he is of the sinister eye, who furnishes most of the backbone to

3. Clipping in Marshall Harvey Twitchell Scrapbook (Microfilm copy in Marshall Harvey Twitchell Papers, Prescott Memorial Library, Louisiana Tech University, Ruston).

his party, and is the impersonation of the devil himself to his political enemies, would ever [*sic*] cease to brood with sleepless vigilance over the deliberations of that body for a sufficient length of time to ever work suspension to the Governor provided even the move had been postponed to the last day of the Senate. Hence it may be clearly infered [*sic*] that as a matter of duty it was right to impeach, but as a political move, it possibly might have and did estop some legislation, that would have proved beneficial to the State and people. . . .

During my early political life in Louisiana I had never taken any notice of the misrepresentations and falsehoods of the local press. The opinion of the public there, I found, was influenced by a man's actions and conduct, not by what the newspapers said, and it did not occur to me that these falsehoods could have any effect on Northern public opinions. I did not think that the North would so readily accept the story of the men who had so lately been in arms against the government and were then, in most cases, barroom loafers and gamblers, in preference to the statement of a man who for four years had fought to sustain the government and was earnestly attempting to support and perpetuate the principles of freedom, for which he had fought.

Absent in the army, I was not familiar with that class of our stay-at-home citizens who were willing that their neighbors' sons should be sacrificed upon the field of battle provided they could by some contract gain profit for themselves by the continuance of the war. These citizens were willing that the rights for which they did not fight, the principles of patriotism which their souls were too small to possess, and the ex-Federal soldier in the South for whom they had no care should all be sacrificed to increase their prospects for Southern trade.

Under the advice of old politicians, I made up my mind to take more notice of these newspaper attacks, and when the Democratic committee was appointed to investigate the charges against United States Senator West, I took occasion to explode an old libel which appeared in the New York *Herald.* From the New Orleans *Republican:*

> As the committee appointed by the Senate to inquire into the manner of Senator West's election never made a report, Senator Twitchell,

4. Ibid.

who was accused by the back biting New York *Herald* of having received a bribe for his vote on that occasion did not have an opportunity to properly vindicate himself. At the request and by the advice of some of his friends, the following correspondence is published:

Senate Chamber,
New Orleans, March 6, 1876.

Senator Robertson, Chairman of Joint Committee to Investigate charges growing out of the election of Hon. J. R. West to the United States Senate:

Sir—The New York *Herald* having charged that I received a bribe for my vote at the election of Hon. J. West to the United States Senate, I now request you to state whether, during the investigation of the joint committee, that charge against myself was sustained, or whether it was alleged by any witness, either directly or by implication, that I received any bribe or other corrupt consideration whatever for my vote on that occasion.

Respectfully, your obedient servant,
M.H. Twitchell.

Senate Chamber,
New Orleans, March 6, 1876.

Hon. M. H. Twitchell, State Senator:

Dear Sir—In reply to your note of this date making a request for information whether, during the investigation of the joint committee to investigate charges growing out of the election of Hon. J. R. West to the United States Senate, any charge was brought against yourself in connection with such election, or whether a charge made against you by the New York *Herald* was sustained or alluded to, I have the honor to state, most emphatically, that no witness who testified before the joint committee either charged or implied in any manner whatever, that you received any bribe or other corrupt consideration for your vote at the election of Hon. J. R. West, and to remain your obedient servant,

W. A. Robertson,
Chairman Joint Committee.[5]

5. Ibid.

21

The Assassination Attempt
and Its Aftermath, 1876

Under the constitution and laws of the state, an election was to
take place in November [1876] for members of the House, governor, lieutenant governor, one half of the other state officers, and
one half of the Senate. The first Monday in January [1877] the old
members of the Senate (a holdover body) would meet in the chamber, the old lieutenant governor presiding, and immediately proceed to complete the quorum of the Senate by swearing in new
members; they would then recognize the House [and], meeting
with it in joint session, the lieutenant governor presiding, receive
the returns and declare the election of the governor, lieutenant
governor, and other officers.

It required the addition of one member to the Senate to make it
complete, for the transaction of business. The holdover senators
were equally divided in politics, but the lieutenant governor, a
Republican, made the Senate practically a Republican body. The
death or inability to attend of a single Republican senator, however, might change the entire result of the election.

A Democratic majority in the old Senate might insist on swearing in Democratic members and setting aside for examination the
credentials of Republican senators, keeping the Senate all the
time Democratic, recognizing a Democratic body as the House,
and declaring the Democratic candidates for governor and state
officers elected.

At the last caucus of Republican senators [in March, 1876, eight
months before the election,] I especially cautioned holdover senators to keep out of the canvass and all places of personal danger,
explaining to them what might be the result if one of them was
assassinated. It did not occur to me that I was at all in danger. I

had become so prominent from the murder of my relatives two years before that I thought the Democrats would consider it wise for them not to again attract public attention to those old murders by another outrage in the same locality and family.

The Democratic leaders, through their happy faculty of making mistakes, listened to the fears of those who had been engaged in the slaughter of my family and decided that I should be the victim, thus quieting the assassins of the Red River districts by the murder of a man from whom they feared prosecution for their previous murders, getting rid of a troublesome Republican leader, and changing the political status of the Senate, and through that, the state.

Immediately after the adjournment of the legislature, I made business arrangements preparatory to spending the summer in the North, as I had fully determined to act myself upon the advice which I gave my colleagues, to be away from the dangers of the political campaign in Louisiana. I well knew that my presence there was of less importance to my political comrades than the chance of my absence would be when the Senate met the first Monday in January.

I reached Starlight the last of April, expecting in a few days to be able to return to the North. On the first of May, I stopped at Coushatta a number of hours later than was my usual custom, and noticing many leaders of the Democratic party coming into town from the country at an unusual time for them, I asked one if he was not a long distance from home for so late an hour. He replied that he had come to see if they couldn't pass a bill which they had been for a long time trying to get through. It did not occur to me at the time that the question whether I was to be shot or not was the bill under consideration.

On the morning of May 2, I started for Coushatta with Mr. King, the last of my Northern brothers-in-law and the one who had escaped assassination two years before on account of his serious illness at the time.[1] As we stepped down to the river and took our places in the skiff, the negro ferryman urged me not to cross that morning, but I was so accustomed to negro timidity that I disregarded his advice and ordered him to pull for the Coushatta shore. Just as we were about to touch the bank I looked up

1. Twitchell gives a somewhat different reason for King's escape in Chap. 18.

from the paper which I was reading and saw a man standing behind a woodpile leveling his rifle at me. I called out, "Down in the boat," and the first shot went over us; then to the ferryman, "Pull back to the other shore." The next shot passed through the skiff and entered my left thigh. I immediately went over into the water, passing under the skiff, and caught hold of the lower edge with my hand, keeping the skiff much of the time between myself and the assassin, while all the time I was partially concealed under the boat and in the water. King, having a revolver, fired two shots at the assassin and was shot dead. One shot at him or me shot the ferryman in the hand.

The assassin was one of the coolest of the kind which the South ever produced; and as a marksman, he was an expert, using his repeating rifle and revolver with such rapidity and accuracy that notwithstanding the poor mark I gave him by the time I had reached the middle of the stream, he succeeded with his last rifle shot in shattering my remaining arm, and I floated on my back away from the skiff. He then fired two shots from his revolver, the last one striking my coat.

Apprehensive that more might follow and hit my body next, I told the ferryman to call out that I was dead. This he promptly did, the words being repeated by ladies on the shore, and the assassin coolly and leisurely mounted his horse and rode away.

The ferryman brought the skiff on the lower side of me, I threw my only uninjured limb on the edge of the boat, and the ferryman, with his unwounded arm, rolled me over into the skiff upon the body of King.

In a few moments I was moved from the skiff to a cabin by my friends. By my directions the commandant and surgeon of the army post were sent for. In a very short time they appeared. I said to Colonel Pennypacker,[2] "I place myself under your protection and request the attendance of your surgeon."

Considering the fact that I had a wound in the back of my neck, a ball in my leg, and each arm shot twice through, I was but very little weakened, for the cold water of the river had so completely chilled me that it stopped the flow of blood which ordinarily would have taken place.

2. Colonel Galusha Pennypacker, commander of the 16th Regiment, Department of the Gulf.

The colonel caused me to be moved at once into a house near his camp, where the next morning my [left] arm was amputated and buried at Starlight with the body of King. For twenty-eight days there was about an even contest for my life, between vitality with good nursing and my many wounds and the warm climate. So severe was the struggle that had I been addicted to the use of whisky, tobacco, or anything weakening to my system, the result would not have been long in doubt. With the exception of Colonel Pennypacker, commanding the camp, I was the only one who did not consider my case hopeless.

I was abundantly supplied by my many friends with wild meat, of which I stood in the greatest need; [I] was lying flat on my back, able to move but one foot, and yet my stomach digested more meat and blood-making food than it ever had before or since in the same length of time.

J. W. Harrison, formerly of the 7th Vermont, under the direction of my sister Helen, took charge of me so far as nursing and guarding the house was concerned. He soon learned of an overheard conversation between the assassin and some friend of his which took place the night after the shooting. The assassin said, "If I had shot the damn nigger, I should have got him, as he would have sunk before anyone could have reached him from the shore." This evidently referred to my being pulled into the boat by the ferryman. There was considerable dissatisfaction between the assassin and the society that employed him. He claimed his pay, and they contended that he had not completed his job.

My foresight in being removed to the camp instead of to my own house was very embarrassing to the assassins. Although in the edge of camp, Mr. Harrison knew the people too well to trust to that for my protection at night; consequently, some trusted friends of undoubted nerve and courage remained in hiding near the house with a Winchester rifle to intercept any prowler who might attempt to murder me. I lacked for nothing in the way of care and attention, although with but two exceptions all offers came from my Republican friends.

My attempted assassination was so purely political that my Democratic friends doubtless felt that their assistance would not be acceptable. I am certain that anything which they would have sent me to eat would have first been tried by the dog.

Mrs. Paxton of Coushatta brought me strawberries from her

garden. She said they threatened to tear up her vines on account of it, but she replied that she had not forgotten to whom she owed her place. Mrs. Paxton's husband, Captain T. E. Paxton (ex-Confederate), a few years before, in the settlement of some case for which he was attorney, found himself short nearly $2,000; it was a matter of honor with him. I loaned him the money, taking a mortgage on his house.

After the riots which were followed by the murder of my brother and others, the Democratic leaders became suspicious that Paxton was not as thoroughly in sympathy with them in the commission of political murders as a man occupying his position and possessing a knowledge of their previous crimes ought to be. He went fishing one day, taking a bottle of whisky supplied by his friends. He was brought home dead. If he had purchased his whisky at a Republican store, his death would not have been so sudden.

Just before I was shot, Mrs. Paxton came to see me and said that she was unable to collect the bills due to her late husband to any such extent as she expected; said she had only $600, which she had come to pay on the mortgage, trusting that I would not turn her and her children outdoors, as she hoped to be able to collect the balance soon. She said that she had been advised by her friends not to pay me at all but let me take the place, that I would receive the money and then turn her outdoors for the balance. I took the six hundred, gave up the notes, and cancelled the mortgage, telling her that she need not distress herself or the children to pay me, that her home was free.

The Mathews family were under much less obligation to me. I had rented a room from the family for a few months and secured a position for the eldest son in the legislature. Miss Mathews and her brother came up from New Orleans, she staying with my sister until I was moved to the city, notwithstanding the disapproval of her Democratic friends.

I look back to these families as the two bright examples of gratitude, rendered brighter by the conduct of others around them. It took no little moral courage at that time for a Democrat to declare himself a friend of the wounded Republican whose death they thought was so certainly but a few days off.

For nearly a month I was encouraged to bear the discomforts of lying in one position by the hope that my right arm might be saved. I know not how long the surgeon had hopes of saving the arm, for I had no doubt of the favorable result until the flesh in the forearm began to decay and I saw them removing the maggots.

On the last day of May, late in the afternoon, the surgeon came into the room, lingering much longer than his custom, evidently dreading the disclosure he was about to make; finally he informed me that the arm could not be saved and that he would take it off in the morning.

I said very well and turned my face to the window, watching the sun as it disappeared behind the trees, reviewing my past life, and trying to imagine what would be my future in the world, without arms and all my near relatives in the grave, except one sister, a mother, and four little boys.

The picture looked so dark and discouraging that I fully made up my mind that life was not worth retaining longer. Sister Helen first recovered her courage and came to my bedside. I said to her, "The surgeon says my right arm must come off, and I do not see any use of living longer." She asked me if I had ever made any money with my hands, and then said, "There are plenty of hands in the world to do the work of heads which have the ability to direct." This gave me a new thought, and in a few moments I had my old-time courage again. The next morning the arm was skillfully amputated, and I started on the road to final recovery.

The day before my arm was amputated, I received a call from a couple of visitors which occasioned a good deal of wonderment among my friends. When I was asked if they should be admitted to the room as they requested, I wondered what they could want. It was midday. I was surrounded by my friends, who were suspicious of them and watching their every movement. I felt that they must know they could not do me harm and escape alive. I concluded that they must have a grudge against some of their comrades and intended to give me some information which might throw suspicion on them. They took seats in the room and engaged in a commonplace conversation for a short time and retired.

I was not long in coming to the correct conclusion as to the object of their visit. The reports of the army surgeon that my recovery was doubtful were discredited, and they desired to learn from what they thought was a more reliable source whether it would be necessary for the assassin to visit me again. They could not have made their call at a better time; the decaying arm, impregnating the room with its disagreeable odour, must have convinced them that in a short time the job would be finished.

The first week in June was fixed by the colored churches of the district as the time for holding a series of meetings in the grove near the military camp. This was my darkest time on account of the weakness from the last amputation. I learned from my friends that the colored people were in attendance at the meetings by the thousands, coming from long distances. I was personally known by the leaders of all north Louisiana. Many of the colored people in that vicinity received from me the first practical knowledge that they were free; it was under my personal supervision and direction that the parish government and courts were organized in which they were recognized as men. It was from my instruction that they first registered and voted. I was the first to break the prejudice of the white people by selling them lands and encouraging them to make homes for themselves; [I] had established and protected their schools, which I still controlled. It was not surprising to me or my friends that the religious meeting should partake much of the character of a prayer meeting for my recovery.

One morning a delegation of colored ministers came, requesting the privilege of being allowed to look at me. The surgeon consented upon the condition that there should be no conversation, as he feared that any excitement would prove fatal. They filed into my room, ranged themselves by my bedside, and stood there with the tears rolling down their cheeks. After repeated questioning, one of them said, "Yes, the colored people are very much excited. We learned yesterday that Major Haney was to be appointed president of the school board as soon as your death, which is expected daily, occurs." Haney was notorious as a drunken gambler, intensely bitter against the colored schools.

My temper was thoroughly aroused at the thought that as soon as life had left my body, the first plan to be carried into effect was to be the checking of civilization by closing the colored schools. I resolved at once to defeat them as long as possible, and told the delegation to return to their people and say that I was going to recover.

In 1874 the murder of Republicans at or near Coushatta and the overturning of state and parish governments by organized mobs had quite a disgusting effect upon the minds of the Democratic leaders in the close Northern states. But the elections of 1874 were over; the fruits of murder and violence had been gathered in. The House of Representatives at Washington and the lower house of the state legislature had thereby become Democratic. As nothing more was to be gained then by further persecution, all was quiet.

The Northern Democratic leader now directed the attention of his simpleminded followers to the quietude of the South as the result of having part of the government in the hands of the Democratic party. They claimed that there would be no more robbery of the people by the legislature of Louisiana, no more interference with the sacred and vested rights of the sovereign states by Congress, no more investigating committees to pry into state affairs and secure perjured testimony for political effect.

When the telegraph informed the people of the North of the murder of King and my attempted assassination, the Democratic Simple Simons ran to their leaders for explanation, and for the first time in the history of their party, the Democratic House passed the following resolution to investigate the Southern outrage, thereby forestalling the Republican Senate and breaking their record of noninterference in state affairs:

> Whereas it is alleged that M. H. Twitchell, a senator of the State of Louisiana and commissioner of the United States court for the State aforesaid, and David King [sic], a citizen of the same State, have been within a few days found murdered on the Red River, in the State aforesaid: Therefore,
>
> *Be it resolved,* That the select committee appointed to investigate the affairs and accounts of the Federal office-holders in the city of New Orleans be, and are hereby, instructed to inquire into the cause of said murder or murders, and that they be authorized to send for persons and enter into a full and complete investigation of the circumstances attending said transaction, and particularly as to whether it was or was not of a political character; and that they report the result of their investigations to this House simultaneously with their other reports.[3]

The above resolution was adopted May 4th, only forty-eight hours after the outrage. By it the chairman of the committee on Louisiana affairs appointed the subcommittee. The chairman was Randall [Lee] Gibson of Louisiana,[4] a man who occupied his posi-

3. *Congressional Record,* 44th Cong., 1st Sess., 3000–3001.
4. Congressman, 1875–83; U.S. senator, 1883–92.

tion as one of the results of the frauds, violence, and murders of the election of 1874. From the Democratic standpoint he was a very proper man to investigate the conduct of his friends, to whom he owed his seat, as they commenced their operations for his reelection.

After waiting impatiently a number of weeks for me to die, the committee, on the 30th of May, adopted the following resolution:

> *Resolved*, That the chairman appoint a subcommittee of two, whose duty it shall be to proceed to Coushatta, on Red River, and make inquiry (as required by resolution of [the] House of Representatives, adopted May 4, 1876) into the cause of the recent murder of David King and wounding of Hon. M. H. Twitchell; also that the subcommittee be authorized to hold sessions at such points in the neighborhood of Coushatta as to them may be deemed necessary to procure evidence in the matter of the proposed inquiry.[5]

Under these resolutions Vance of Ohio (a Democrat)[6] and Woodburn of Nevada[7] reached Coushatta June 6th. They came to my room and read a number of questions which they wished to ask me, saying that they wanted to learn the whole truth and desired to commence with my testimony. I recognized the questions as having been furnished by the local politicians of Coushatta and asked Mr. Vance to read the resolution under which he was making the investigation. The resolution was read. I remarked that it was all right, but from his questions I thought it should read that they had come there to try me for being shot. This remark was an evident surprise and disturbance to the committee. They finally promised that if any testimony appeared against me personally, that I should have an opportunity of calling rebutting witnesses, and that on account of my condition all such testimony should be brought to me for examination.

I was much to blame for trusting these promises. I should have known that they were only given to deceive me and secure my testimony; honor, honesty, or decency were qualifications which would have perfectly unfitted the committee for the work which they were to perform.

5. *House Reports*, 44th Cong., 1st Sess., No. 816, vi.
6. John Luther Vance, congressman, 1875–77.
7. William Woodburn, Republican congressman, 1875–77, 1885–89.

For three days the investigation was continued on the line of trying King and me for being shot. General Mudgett, representing my interests, was allowed to cross-examine a few of the witnesses; but as he succeeded in getting from each, in substance, that I was shot for political causes, the committee refused to allow him to proceed, giving as an excuse that they had not the time. The examination was most remarkable in many respects. Witnesses were selected who in most cases were so implicated in the murder of my friends in 1874 that they felt that their lives were at stake in swearing away my political influence; Republicans were selected from the weak, poor, discontented, and timid, who hoped from their testimony to be allowed to live there in peace.

Instead of showing me the testimony as promised, they took special care to keep it from me or my friends, leaving for New Orleans in the night, taking their most extravagant witnesses on the boat, and examining them on the way down the river when they were absolutely certain of no Republican oversight.

After—or before—the taking of this testimony, a report was formulated and, with such a portion of the evidence as they thought desirable, given to Congress. This report, stripped of its generalities and meaningless verbiage contained the following charges:

> The testimony of all the disinterested witnesses . . . in regard to the conduct of parochial affairs [in Red River Parish] was to the effect that they had been loosely and extravagantly managed, and that Mr. Twitchell was responsible for their mismanagement. Numerous instances were cited showing a profligate waste of public money.
>
> The lands of the parish were assessed at figures largely in excess of their value, and of the assessment in the neighboring parishes. . . . In many cases absolute confiscation resulted.
>
> It became necessary to erect a court-house. . . . Twitchell . . . caused the building to be erected and reaped the profit therefrom. Although the contract was let at $16,525, yet the evidence goes to show that, in reality, the work has cost upward of $40,000.
>
> Again, Mr. Twitchell procured the building of several levees, and the evidence shows that gross frauds were perpetrated upon the treasury, and large sums of money realized therefrom by Twitchell and his confederates.

Your committee cannot, within the space of this report, recapitulate the worse than profligate conduct of school affairs, and other irregularities and malpratices of Mr. Twitchell and his associates. . . .

Your committee . . . are of the opinion . . . that the shooting of King and Twitchell was not caused by reason of their political opinions, and that the affair "was not of a political character."[8]

I will consider the last conclusion of the committee first. It was one which the Democratic party had decided upon before the investigation, a conclusion which they must have to enable them to excuse the other outrages which had taken place and those which they knew would take place in the campaign just commenced.

In the testimony printed I find that three Republicans testified that the assault was political. Ten Democrats and conservatives declared that it was not political. Twenty witnesses of different parties were not asked the question. It was among the last pronounced. If the witness, by his previous testimony, indicated too great a degree of truthfulness and caution, the question was omitted; but if [he was] reckless and extravagant, it was asked, and ten times out of thirteen they received the desired answer.

Of the ten who said that the shooting was not of a political character, six had been arrested for the murder of my relatives and friends in 1874 and were prepared to testify to anything to assist the Democratic party, as through its influence alone could they hope to escape punishment for the murders committed. Of the remaining four the only one entitled to consideration, one of the brightest businessmen of Coushatta, testified that I was perfectly honorable in business, my work unquestioned everywhere, and could be trusted perfectly in everything except politics; and yet he declared that my attempted assassination was not of a political character.

A few feeble attempts were made to prove that I had personal enemies who might have shot me. This failed and they were compelled to fall back upon the only other cause given, which was that I had such great political influence that I controlled everything; and yet the committee declared in substance that my shooting was not for political purposes.

The next charge was that the parochial affairs had been loosely

8. *House Reports*, 44th Cong., 1st Sess., No. 816, viii–ix.

and extravagantly managed. If they had searched the books, which were at their disposal in the building where they examined their witnesses, they might have stricken out "loosely" and discovered just where the extravagance was and who was responsible for the outlay.

Their examination was most remarkable when they had before them a witness who knew all about the parish affairs and was perfectly familiar with the records. They kept his answers, by their system of questioning, away from the records and doings of which he had such positive knowledge; but when they had an ignorant man who knew nothing of parish proceedings except from hearsay, nothing of the books, had never seen them in many instances, could not have read them if he had, this witness was just the one which they would question at the greatest length and whose opinion about the management of affairs they were most desirous of getting.[9]

There were two years in which there was great extravagance, if not criminality, in the sheriff's office (an officer elected by the people), which we were unable to check for some time. This sheriff had a plan of encouraging complaints against the planters by their hands. He would influence the laborer to swear out a warrant, getting the names of a large number of witnesses, and then ride up to the plantation, serve the warrant, and subpoena all at the same time, but would charge the parish with the full mileage of each paper separately, thereby getting for one journey of perhaps 20 miles, mileage for 200; then the case, which he knew was trivial from the start, was allowed to drop.

Our district attorney, by my request, thoroughly investigated one of his bills against the parish and reported that he believed an indictment would hold against the sheriff. A few days after this, the sheriff was shot and wounded by a Mr. Gillem for an official irregularity from which Mr. Gillem was the sufferer. After consultation with the district attorney and prominent citizens of the parish without regard to party, it was thought best to let the sheriff resign and not press the charges against him.

This old sheriff, John T. Yates, who credited me with being the party who led the crusade against his stealing and forced his resig-

9. The testimony referred to here and in the pages that follow: *ibid.*, 645–727.

nation, was the independent whose testimony was just bristling with [accounts of] my irregularities and official crimes.

While sheriff, he was also postmaster, as he told the committee; but he neglected to tell them that the U.S. marshal had made earnest efforts to get hold of him for two years for an explanation of the disappearance of registered letters and postage stamps which could be traced no further than the Coushatta post office.

A thorough investigation would have proven that there was no extravagance in parochial affairs where I had had any control. I was blamed by the committee for an extravagant assessment of the lands of the parish, from which in some cases actual confiscation occurred. The three officers constituting the board of assessors were elected by the people. In common with the 1,300 Republican voters of the parish, I voted for them and that much was responsible for their action. The chairman of the board testified before the committee that I had no control over them. The fact appeared in testimony that I was North during the entire time the assessment was being made. One witness contended that I did all the mischief by giving the board of assessors my assessment before I left. I did tell the chairman that I should not complain at his proposal to assess my plantation at $12,000. I had paid a few years before $21,000 in cash for the place and could not say to the assessor that its taxable value was less than $12,000.

When I returned from the North, one of the witnesses complained to me of the assessment made during my absence and asked if there was no relief, as he thought that it was higher than in other portions of the state and that thereby we would have to pay more than our proportion of the state tax. After looking up the law, we found that there was no relief except by special legislation. When the legislature met, I compared the assessment of the parish with others in the state and found it was among the lowest instead of the highest. I did not need to consult with anyone to come to the conclusion that the less I said about inequalities of assessment the better it would be for my parish.

Some lands were actually sold for taxes under an act which I introduced into the legislature and perhaps caused its passage. I found that there were large quantities of land which were never given in to the assessment board, thereby escaping taxation. Nobody claiming to own them, they could neither be taxed nor purchased. In common with others, I used my influence to have them put upon the assessment roll to "unknown owners."[10] Some of these lands were sold, but most of them, upon being advertised, brought forth an owner, who paid the taxes and released the land.

The next finding of the committee against me is that I built the courthouse and "reaped the profit therefrom." I did not build the courthouse and had nothing to do with the profits if there were any. As president of the police jury, I had much to do with it, from which I have no pleasant recollections. The legislature authorized the parish to issue $20,000 in "bonds for the building of the Court House and other purposes." It was my duty to have these bonds prepared, sold, and the money placed in the treasury. To prevent their going too low and to give confidence to other purchasers, I bid off $5,000 of the bonds. The preparation, advertising, sale at public auction, delivery of the bonds, and payment of the money into the treasury were all matters of public record.

When the order from the Democratic campaign committee came, that all the leading Republicans must be indicted for an effect upon public opinion of the North, I was absent from the parish; but my Democratic friends caused the indictment to be for the embezzlement of those bonds, because, as they said, the public records would themselves disprove the charge.

The voluble witness, Yates, took the contract for the building of the courthouse and carried it out in part, Lisso Brothers, both Democrats, furnishing him the means. One of the firm came to me and said they were afraid of Yates's honesty and that if the contract could not be changed so that the money might be paid direct to them instead of through Yates, they would stop furnishing the subcontractors.

Yates transferred the contract to Lisso Brothers. I do not remember how it was done, but I presume there was some truth in his testimony about the matter. As chief executive officer of the parish, deeply interested in the completion of the public buildings, I may have advised him to transfer the contract.

A. B. Broughton[11] indicated his willingness to testify that the courthouse cost $65,000. This seemed a little too extravagant for the committee's use, and it dropped to $40,000; so far as his ac-

10. *Acts of the State of Louisiana,* 1873, p. 100.
11. Republican parish judge.

tual knowledge was concerned, it was unnecessary for him to have made any change in his testimony.

Julius Lisso,[12] Democratic parish treasurer, a man of ability and unquestionable knowledge about the courthouse contract and parish money affairs, and a man of too much character to make statements which could at once be disproved by the public records, testified that Yates took the courthouse contract and that Lisso Brothers advanced him the money to carry it out, for which they were to have one half the profits of the contract; that just before settlement Yates came in and told them to make settlement with me for his portion of the contract. His extravagance in personal expenses was fully equal to his extravagance in testifying; he never failed to borrow wherever and whenever he could and never made a payment which he could avoid.

Mr. Lisso testified, to the annoyance of the committee, that the $22,600 in warrants of which Broughton spoke was not an additional payment but simply drafts on him as parish treasurer for the money which he had in the treasury. But very few of the witnesses were familiar enough with business to understand that a warrant on the treasury or a cheque on the bank should not be added to cash drawn to ascertain the amount paid for the article. Mr. Lisso knew it and corrected in part Mr. Broughton's testimony. The committee knew it and saw the mistake of the witnesses, but for political purposes they preferred to follow the mistake.

The committee closed their charge against me [by alleging that I made] "large sums of money" from "the building of several levees" and managed the school affairs with profligacy and irregularity. I must confess that I was very much surprised after thoroughly searching the testimony to find how little this very able committee required upon which to base the most serious charges. They must have been in condition to see more than double when they reviewed the testimony referring to levees and school affairs.

The voluble Yates, who could not remember that he built the courthouse, although one [member] of the Democratic firm who furnished him the money had a distinct recollection of it, the Yates, who as postmaster forgot to deliver registered letters or

12. The other Lisso brother, Marks (probably Marx), died of yellow fever in 1873.

make return for stamps received, remembered anything which the committee might require referring to irregularities or profligacy [of mine].

There was another witness who, the night after I was shot, bitterly complained to someone, who from the darkness my informer could not recognize, [that] because he [the assassin] did not shoot the d—— nigger first, Twitchell had gotten away. This witness was willing to testify to irregularities in school affairs.

To understand the testimony, one must know the character of the Republican officials eighteen months before and [of] the seizure of the government by the very parties who—a second time by murder—seemed to be again in power and, with a committee of their own, were looking up excuses for the violence committed. Assassins testified in their own favor and blackened the character of their victims. Former Republicans of weak character, with spirits broken, lent their assistance to be freed from further persecution.

Some Democrats of character were examined, but without exception they knew nothing wrong, except from hearsay, and, when referring to my personal character, expressed the most perfect confidence in my integrity and honesty. The truth is that the state of affairs was then, as well as now, very different from any law-abiding Northern community.

All of the complaints contained in the testimony of irregularities and offences occurred before the overturning of the parish government eighteen months previous under officers elected by the people, over whom I had no control. To supply the place of these murdered officers and again establish civil government in place of being ruled by a mob, I did cause the appointment of new officers who were, at the time the committee was in the parish, in charge of the government.

I think I was the only man in the parish who kept a bank account in New Orleans, the capital of the state. Perhaps for this reason and the opinion of the people, without regard to politics, that I was reliable and honest, settlements with the state treasurer in New Orleans as well as other parties, and the paying out of moneys in the parish of Red River by levee contractors and others, were made through me, thereby avoiding the danger and expense of transporting money to and from the city. I have yet to learn that there has been any claim of loss by anyone therefrom.

The inference which might be drawn from the report of the committee, that the management of school and levee affairs had anything to do with increasing the taxpayers' burdens of the parish, is very erroneous. The school tax was levied by the state, made up largely of the poll tax, and was collected from the parishes whether their school affairs were managed good or bad. The levee tax was collected also by the state and paid into the state treasury.

It had been a standing complaint of the parishes back from the Mississippi River that they had always been taxed for the benefit of the rich Mississippi River planter. I took this matter up, and for the first time in the history of the Red River valley, quite an extensive series of levees were built, increasing largely the value of the lands.

It must have been considered by the Democratic planter a strange irony of fate that these almost incalculable benefits to the parish, without the slightest expense to anyone in it, should have been counted by the committee as one of the burdens resting upon the people for which I was responsible. It was a burden upon the Democratic party, and they could find no way of getting rid of it except to kill the man whom the people considered had given them these benefits.

Levee contracts were all made and settled in New Orleans. An investigation of the records there would have shown that I built no levees [and] had no connection with them except to urge their construction for the benefit of the district which I represented. A further examination of the contractors might have developed that I acted as their banker at Coushatta in paying the orders of the subcontractors.

There was much prejudice at first against white teachers for colored schools. Some of them came to me and said that merchants would no longer credit them for the necessaries which they must have while teaching. To help them out of this dilemma, I advised them to sign blank receipts for their pay and deposit them with the merchants for security; and I would then assure the merchants that I would sign the order on the school treasury, which was a part of the receipt, after the term of school was completed. The receipt was left blank as to amount because we never knew at what time the chivalry might conclude to burn the schoolhouse, whip and drive out the teacher, or in some other manner close the school. Under the oversight of the public schools by the state school board, it would have been impossible, without detection, to have filled one of those orders, which went into the school treasury, with a different amount from that which was in the contract and on file in the office of the president of the school board.

I understand that there was much bitterness against me on account of the public schools [in other respects]. By threatening that I, as president of the school board, should refuse to sign the warrant for the payment of the teacher of the white school in any ward in which the colored school was broken up, I had forced them to the disagreeable duty of keeping their rowdies in check and protecting the colored schools. The first school treasurer was murdered in 1874. George A. King, his successor, was killed at the time I was shot; for my own protection, as I was his bondsman, I carried the records to New Orleans. In 1877, after the Democrats were in full possession of all departments of the state government, a committee was appointed by the legislature to investigate the school affairs of the different parishes in the state. I placed before them the entire records of the school board of the parish of Red River for the whole time that I was connected with the board. The following is their report:

Red River parish. Senator M. H. Twitchell appeared before the committee and being sworn stated that having ascertained that there was no report from the Parish of Red River, and having been the bondsman of G. A. King and H. J. Twitchell, both of whom are now dead, he desired to furnish such information as was in his possession. He produced twenty-three vouchers of amounts paid by King as Treasurer, from Nov. 6, 1874, to Feb. 6, 1876, amounting in all to the sum of $2893.78. He further states that after King's death, he as his bondsman, settled with his successor J. W. Harrison. The report of this settlement was indorsed on the books of the treasurer. The vouchers aforesaid were examined by the committee and found correct.

The witness further produced sixty-seven vouchers paid by H. J. Twitchell, treasurer, from July 11, 1871, to July 6, 1874, amounting to the sum of $9330.83 and also the relinquishment of Wm. C. Brown, State Superintendent of public education, for the balance outstanding against said Twitchell as treasurer at the time of his death, $2393.07, the same being in pursuance to Act No. 31 of the year 1875.

N. H. Ogden,
Chairman of Committee.[13]

The Democratic committee sent to New Orleans, with Randall [Lee] Gibson as its chairman, was for the purpose of procuring the testimony of Republican mismanagement of official affairs in Louisiana for political use in the coming campaign. In appointing such a committee, the Democratic speaker, true to his party interests, would naturally appoint Republicans who would give the majority just as little trouble as possible in formulating a report; necessarily, some of the weakest men in the Republican party would here find their place.

When Mr. Gibson was called upon to appoint a subcommittee, he selected for its chairman Mr. Vance of Ohio, who had the session before proved his peculiar fitness for the position by making a report against the public printer at Washington in which he so overdid his work that it was necessary to have it done again, thereby causing the public printer to be relieved from all [suspicion of] irregularity and dishonesty. My case was quite different. The parties to be vilified were dead or thought to be dying. Coushatta, unlike the public printing office, was a long way from Washington, and Mr. Vance was thought to be just the man. Later he showed his fitness for the work by his conduct, as given below in the Democratic *Evening Star* of Washington, April 3, 1878:

EX-CONGRESSMAN VANCE. HE RAN OFF WITH $15,000
and ANOTHER MAN'S WIFE.
New York, April 3. A Cincinnati special says: Gentlemen who arrived here yesterday afternoon from Gallipolis, Ohio, state that Col. Vance, before leaving home, borrowed large sums of money from his relatives and business acquaintances. The amount that he succeeded in obtaining is estimated to be not less than $15,000, and it may reach $20,000. His two brothers-in-law, who are now in pursuit of him, are among the losers. It is reported by the gentlemen from

13. The editor was unable to locate the original of this document. Note, however, that act *31* has been substituted for act *35* in the last line (*Acts of the State of Louisiana*, 1875, pp. 69–71).

Gallipolis that there is a woman in the case. About the time Col. Vance left home the wife of a music teacher, who is famous for her personal charms, also disappeared. Her name had been connected with that of Col. Vance by current gossip, but the stories were not believed by the latter's friends. The woman has been heard from at St. Louis, whither Vance is known to have gone, and facts are being developed daily which go to show that the two have taken flight together. Col. Vance is connected by marriage with one of the most respectable families in southeastern Ohio, and has hitherto borne an unsullied reputation. His credit was so high in Cincinnati that he could have obtained large sums of money had he given himself time. The developments of the past day cause great excitement among his personal friends here.[14]

The appointment of Woodburn, the so-called Republican member of the committee, was evidently not a mistake, viewing the question from a Democratic standpoint. In the committee room at Coushatta, Republicans continually mistook him for the Democratic member, as he, to all appearances, was the most zealous in obtaining testimony which might blacken the character of the Republicans. He would promptly stop a witness if he chanced to speak of the murder of Republican officials committed eighteen months before, with the remark that they were not investigating that matter, while he questioned, without limit as to time, any witness who showed a disposition to say anything against the parties murdered, seeming then to forget that he was not investigating that case. I presume he felt that he must satisfy his employers that he was earning his money.

Woodburn is reported to have been an expert poker player and to have won large amounts at Coushatta before signing the report. Winning money at poker before favorable official action is a matter well understood by Southern politicians.

14. Clipping in Marshall Harvey Twitchell Scrapbook (Microfilm copy in Marshall Harvey Twitchell Papers, Prescott Memorial Library, Louisiana Tech University, Ruston).

22

Death in Indianapolis, 1876

The last of June, after urgent requests from myself and friends,
Dr. Carson decided to move me to New Orleans. Under his care
and protected by a military guard, I was taken onto the boat,
reaching the city about the 1st of July. The Democratic leaders
were very much chagrined and annoyed at my persistency in
clinging to life; they felt that my death was absolutely necessary
for their future peace and safety. This was well understood by my
friends, and my removal from Springville to the boat was at a very
early hour, wholly unexpected by the people. My arrival at New
Orleans and removal to the house where rooms had been engaged
was also carefully planned and carried out. A little delay at the
door, in dismissing the soldiers and arranging the stretcher so that
it would enter, gave opportunity for a small crowd to assemble.
Just as I was carried in, I heard one of the crowd say, "What a pity
they did not finish him up the river." At New Orleans it became
painfully observant that the repeated nervous shocks to which
my sister Helen had been subjected for the preceding two years
had completely undermined her health, and I hurried my depar-
ture for the North.

At the depot in Indianapolis we were met by my old friend and
army comrade C. W. Smith, Esq., and immediately taken to his
house. Here we received every attention which sympathetic kindness could suggest, surrounded by a community which had
reached a plane of civilization not to be attained by a people de-
based by the degrading influence of human slavery. The difference
in our position and surroundings may be faintly comprehended
from my sister's exclamations in her half-delirious moments. She
would raise herself from her bed in the greatest fright, but upon

recognizing the faces of some of the kind family, falling back on her pillows, would remark with a smile, "We are safe here. You are Marshall's friends."

When we halted at Indianapolis, it was my intention to stay over Sunday and then go on to our place in Vermont. Monday came and Mrs. Willis [Helen] was unable to travel. My sister Helen was one of those combinations of a strong mind with a weak body. The family had always recognized her mental power and brightness as being little short of genius. On account of her physical weakness she was generally relieved as much as possible from violent exercise. These continual attentions, instead of rendering her selfish, gave her the strongest attachment for the different members of her family. She hated falsehood and treachery in all of their forms and had a great admiration for truth, honor, and honesty. Had the evil genius of the universe selected one of the family who would have suffered the most and the keenest from the treachery, falsehood, and dishonesty of the Southern chivalry, sister Helen would have been the one chosen.

For the two years preceding, the full powers of her mind had been called into requisition. Her husband had been murdered in cold blood, after she had persuaded him to give up his gun and submit to arrest. Her surroundings and the necessity for action were such that physical powers could be given neither rest nor relaxation. One of her brothers and two brothers-in-law had been murdered. Her only [surviving] sister, dying of yellow fever, had been cared for by her and the negroes; finally, I had been shot and rendered helpless. During these two years she had had almost the entire oversight of our property in Louisiana, managing it with a success unequaled by anyone. I have no doubt that it was the feeling of responsibility resting upon her which enabled her to carry the load without breaking down. At Indianapolis, for the first time she found herself surrounded by friends and felt that I could be cared for without her help. The repeated shocks to her nerves were more than she could longer endure; the system relaxed, and she had not the strength to recover but, in a few days, passed away to that rest which she had so long desired, where the innocent sleep of childhood no longer required a guard and where prisoners disarmed with solemn pledges of protection could no longer be murdered by Southern chivalry.

I do not think that I am lacking in affection for my friends and relatives, but the manner in which they were taken away, the venom of the Southern press, and the fact that so many people of both races were looking to me for protection, support, and encouragement dried up the fountain of my tears; and every fresh outrage but stimulated me to greater exertions for the acquisition of wealth and power for the punishment of the wrongdoers. Until I was rendered so helpless by their last attack, I firmly believed that right would finally prevail and that I would see the murderers legally punished for their crimes in the judicial district where those crimes were committed. When informed that Helen was dead, that the last of my family was gone, the only hands which I could trust to do my bidding powerless in death, I fully recognized that justice for the murders of my family would never be done, and for the first time tears came to my relief.

Indianapolis recognized the funeral as one of importance. Reverend Dr. Bayliss, pastor of Trinity M[ethodist] E[piscopal] Church, conducted the service, which opened with singing of the hymn "Oh, for the death of those Who slumber in the Lord." Following the hymn Reverend Dr. Gillett led in a very touching and fervent prayer, in which he invoked the protection of Almighty God upon the surviving relative of the deceased, who had been called to pass through a suffering almost unparalleled but which might be sanctified not only to his benefit but to the good of the nation, which must sooner or later learn to do justice and work [for] righteousness. Reverend Dr. Bayliss read the 56th Psalm and the fourteenth chapter of the Gospel according to St. John, after which the chorus sang "To thee, O God, when creatures fail, Thy flock, deserted, flies."

It was one of the complaints of Southern Democrats that Northern men [who] settled in the South did not identify themselves sufficiently with the interests of the country, many of them unmarried and leasing lands, with no business except politics and the governing of the country by the manipulation of the colored vote. I had married a daughter of one of the influential Southern aristocratic families, who all became my friends and supporters. In addition to this, my entire family, with wives and children and all the property which they possessed, had moved South and were engaged in building up the country.

So different was our case that at the Coushatta riot the major-general of the White League tried to get orders through to the guard not to allow the men to be killed but to bring them safely to Shreveport. As this organization was purely political, I have always been satisfied that it was not the desire of the state leaders to have me assassinated, as they foresaw the political injury it would be; but they were unable to control the assassins of the Red River district.

No act of the White League gave the Democratic party more trouble than my attempted assassination. Coushatta, from previous murders, had a very bad reputation. King, my last Northern brother-in-law, was killed, while I was so badly shot that even my political enemy was forced to sympathize. I was moved down the Red River with a United States guard which attracted much attention, then up through the country to Indianapolis [in] one of the pivotal states, where my last sister died.

This was the midsummer of 1876. The presidential nominations had taken place. Indiana was a close state. For the Democratic party no place could have been more unfortunate than Indianapolis for the closing scene of Helen's life. The Democratic papers, disregarding decency or humanity, struggled vigorously to offset the effect upon the public mind. The following from the Indianapolis *Sentinel*, is a sample: "As soon as one of the old broken down streetcar horses sent here . . . to recuperate, dies, from outrages committed upon it in the South, Brother Bayliss will be engaged for a funeral harangue. . . ."[1]

The Democratic papers, in their frantic efforts to save their party, and ignorant of my character, were continually making the matter worse. One paper claimed that the Twitchell family were negroes; another that I was intemperate. Such charges, so generally known to be false, reacted upon the papers, destroying their credibility in other respects. One paper charged me with being a coward in the army. This brought the published statement of Colonel O. A. Bartholomew, as follows:

> In view of the above statements, and the fact that Senator Twitchell, during the two last years of the war, was a captain, serving continually in the regiment of which I was Colonel and commanding, I

1. Clipping in Marshall Harvey Twitchell Scrapbook (Microfilm copy in Marshall Harvey Twitchell Papers, Prescott Memorial Library, Louisiana Tech University, Ruston).

desire to do him the justice to deny every such statement. Capt. Twitchell was, in the strictest sense of the word, a good man; gentlemanly, kind and courteous, and no man was braver than he, and it is a slander upon the character of a fearless soldier, whose record in twenty hard fought battles, attest his bravery to charge him with cowardice.

Yours,
O. A. Bartholomew[2]

As I left the West, where I was comparatively unknown, and travelled east to Vermont, the newspaper attacks changed. I was no longer a negro nor of bad military record; my family [was] not disreputable. They confined themselves to the testimony of the witnesses before the congressional committee. Some of these newspaper articles I answered, but soon tired of the useless work. I knew that it would take a long time to make the people of New England understand that truthfulness, integrity, and honesty were words having a meaning as different in the South as slavery was from freedom. Perjury [in the South] could not be committed in a political case. Testimony was purchasable, and then a retraction could be bought by the other side, as in the case of E. L. Weber, their state witness.[3] It is an accepted maxim in the South that all is fair in politics.

Soon after the death of sister Helen [on] August 12, I left for my home in Vermont. My mother I found sick in bed. She was a woman of wonderful strength, had endured the death of her husband, two daughters, the murder of her youngest son, her three sons-in-law, and my attempted assassination with heroic fortitude; but the death of her last daughter in Indianapolis, with the knowledge that I was returning in a helpless condition, was more than she could bear.

The bullet which I received in the left leg lodged between the large artery and the nerve on the inside; the surgeon had thought

2. *Ibid.*
3. Weber was an important witness before the 1878 House investigating committee chaired by New York Democrat Clarkson N. Potter and generally known as the Potter Commission. An apostate Republican, Weber accused Twitchell and other Louisiana senators of having run a bribery ring during Reconstruction. Twitchell denied the allegation and labeled Weber a perjurer; he gives the controversy extensive coverage in his scrapbook (*ibid.*).

best not to disturb it. Changing its position one day onto the nerve, it caused me to fall. Dr. Gale of Brattleboro was sent for and removed it nicely, but the leg has never fully recovered.

Under the healthful surroundings of my Vermont home, I gained rapidly. In company with J. W. Harrison, who came with me from the South, I visited the Philadelphia Centennial for the purpose of finding the best artificial arms in use. My recovery had an encouraging effect upon my mother, and she was soon again caring for what there was left of her five children—an armless son and three little grandsons.[4]

October 26, I married in South Wilbraham, [Massachusetts,] Miss Henrietta Cushman Day, my sweetheart of Leland Seminary. This was described as one of the great social events of the village of South Wilbraham. The beauty and popularity of the bride, added to the national notoriety of the groom, would not permit the occasion to be one of ordinary importance.

My uncle, Colonel Jonas Twitchell, the last one of my father's generation, was old and feeble. He very earnestly requested that I should remove my father's remains from the village cemetery and my sister Helen's from Corn Hill cemetery, Indiana, to the Twitchell cemetery in Townshend. Under the circumstances I could not resist his appeal. In a few months, as he anticipated, he passed away.

4. There were four Twitchell grandsons, but one of them, Homer Jonas, Jr., presumably lived with his mother, Marshall's sister-in-law, Lottie Miller Twitchell.

23

Again in New Orleans, 1877

The last of December, I left the North with my wife for New Orleans, to be there for the meeting of the legislature the first Monday in January [1877]. The Republican leaders had been killed or driven out and the voters so intimidated that the Democrats had succeeded in getting into the ballot boxes a majority of votes. The only thing which stood in their way was the state returning board, which was created for just such an emergency. The constitution of the state made each house the sole judge of the qualifications of its members. It also provided that after a gubernatorial election the two houses should meet in joint session and declare the vote for governor. He then stepped forward and took the oath of office, then returned to the executive chamber and received a committee from the Senate and a committee from the House, and the government was complete.

The returning board, as required by law, threw out [the votes of] districts where the evidence was beyond question that there had been no fair election. The result of the election so declared by the returning board gave the electoral vote of the state to [Rutherford B.] Hayes; and by a larger majority Packard,[1] the Republican nominee for governor, was elected with a Republican legislature. It was the tactics of the Democrats to dispute everything and declare that they had carried the election from the top to the bottom.

I knew that the first Monday in January the very existence of a Republican government in Louisiana would depend upon the nine

1. Stephen B. Packard, United States marshal in the state for most of Reconstruction.

holdover Republican senators being in their places in the Senate chamber, so that with the aid of the lieutenant governor presiding, the swearing in of new Democratic senators could be delayed until [enough other Republicans had arrived that] the nine holdover Republicans had a majority and a quorum.

I had calculated correctly that my train would reach New Orleans at ten a.m. of the day that the legislature met, but by some management of the Southern politicians and the railroads, the train was three hours late. I at once drove to the State House and found the Senate in session, a Republican senator talking against time, waiting for my arrival, when the swearing in of Republicans would commence by the Republican majority which we possessed in the casting vote of the lieutenant governor.

As I entered the chamber, senators crowded around me, the proceedings stopped, and a recess of five minutes declared. My comrades of the Senate, who had not seen me since the amputation of my arms, tried to greet me pleasantly, but the tears flowed. Senator White, now on the supreme bench,[2] was one of the first Democratic senators to speak to me or to make the attempt; his emotions would not allow him to speak, and he returned to his own side of the chamber. The arrival of one man, or part of a man, changed the entire programme.

The legislature was organized, the state government declared, and a United States senator, Governor W. P. Kellogg, elected, thereby giving the Senate of the United States a Republican majority of one. The Democrats, as soon as they found themselves beaten, withdrew and formed another government,[3] which existed until April, when by a compromise the two governments came together, Democratic in all its branches; and on April 23, I took my seat in the Senate with the other Republicans who were recognized as elected by both parties.[4]

2. Edward Douglass White, associate justice of the United States Supreme Court from 1894 to 1910 and chief justice from 1910 to 1921.

3. A more accurate version of events is that armed Metropolitan Police announced that only those Democrats deemed elected by the Republican returning board should be admitted to the State House. Rejecting this, the Democrats established a rival legislature.

4. The situation in Louisiana was part of the larger crisis of the disputed presidential election of 1876 that led to the so-called Compromise of 1877. By April Hayes had been inaugurated as president, and the larger national questions basi-

This trouble left me much poorer than I was, as I could not understand how President Hayes could accept the vote of Louisiana and fail to sustain Governor Packard, who received more votes than he did. I had been in my position but a short time when I discovered that about one-half of the Democratic majority of the Senate was opposed to the compromise which had been made, and that to carry it out faithfully, the help of the Republicans was necessary.

As the leader of my faction in the Senate, I came in contact quite often with Governor Nicholls,[5] a Confederate veteran who had lost one leg and one arm. I remember him among a few of the Southern Democrats who always kept his word with me.

That winter[6] a commission from Washington visited New Orleans for the purpose of harmonizing the conflicting interests and doing away with one of the state governments. As a representative from one of the Senates, I met them quite often. Mr. Harlan, now justice on the supreme bench,[7] and Senator Hawley[8] impressed me as being good Republicans and honest men of superior ability. Wayne MacVeagh in all respects gave me just the opposite

---

cally settled. In New Orleans the Democratic government of Governor Francis R. T. Nicholls grew stronger daily while that of his Republican rival, Stephen B. Packard, grew weaker. The Republicans could not survive without the protection of federal troops, and Hayes was determined that such protection should be withdrawn. The problem was how to remove the troops without inviting Democratic retaliation against the loyal Louisiana Republicans, perhaps even bringing on another bloody massacre.

In late March Hayes had appointed a special presidential commission headed by Wayne MacVeagh, a Pennsylvania Republican, to go to New Orleans and work out a settlement. The compromise referred to here by Twitchell was the conclusion of the MacVeagh commission's work. In brief, duly elected Republicans, as well as a number of radicals whose seats were contested, were allowed to take their seats in the Nicholls legislature. The Democrats promised to abide by the Thirteenth, Fourteenth, and Fifteenth Amendments, and to provide for Negro education. They further promised not to retaliate against the Republicans. Accepting these pledges, Hayes ordered the troops back to their barracks, and Reconstruction was over.

5. Francis R. Tillou Nicholls, Confederate general and twice governor of Louisiana, from 1877 to 1880 and from 1888 to 1892.

6. "Spring" would be more accurate; the commission arrived in New Orleans on April 5.

7. John Marshall Harlan of Kentucky served as an associate justice of the Supreme Court from 1877 to 1911.

8. Actually, Joseph Roswell Hawley of Connecticut was still a Congressman; he was not elected to the Senate until 1881.

impression. I wondered then, as I have many times since, why he was ever appointed by a Republican administration to an important position.

After the closing of the legislature I returned to the North. President Hayes promised me an appointment in the government service as soon as the next session of the legislature adjourned. The presence of the Republican senators was considered absolutely necessary to aid the conservative senators and the governor in carrying out the agreement which had been made, that the courts should not be used for the persecution of the Republicans.

I spent the summer North and returned to New Orleans for the meeting of the legislature the first Monday in January, 1878. Having been accustomed to revolutions, the session seemed tame and uninteresting. I stopped at Washington on my return to the North and on the first day of April was appointed consul at Kingston, Canada. Kingston was selected because there was little to do; it was near my former home and in all respects was thought to be a comfortable place for me to stay during the short time which they considered I had to live. People have always been deceived about my vitality.

The time between the date of my appointment and the first of May, when I was to take charge of my office, I spent in Newfane and Townshend amidst the scenes of my boyhood and surrounded by my early friends. At first it was very agreeable, but soon I began to tire of the perfect peace, safety, and lack of excitement and danger in those New England villages.

Many a time I thought, what a change from seventeen years before, when I left New England a smooth-faced boy as a private in the 4th Vermont Regiment. From private, without military education, I had fought my way to a captaincy. Without experience in government, no one to advise with, and with only a few lines as my instructions, I successfully established and carried on for nine months the government of a parish, with the record of but one homicide.

With only a few months study in the law office of Judge Roberts,[9] no experience in political management or legislative action, no experience as a merchant or planter, I had creditably filled

9. In Chapter 2, Twitchell states that he had studied law in the office of a Judge Shafter.

offices and positions as member of the constitutional convention, justice of the peace, president of the parish school board, parish judge, United States commissioner, and member of the state Senate; while by the erection of mills, stores, and the purchasing of plantations, I had accumulated a fortune of at least $100,000. In two years this had all gone, and with it my only brother, my three sisters and their husbands, and both of my arms. A life of success, failure, and tragedy, all in seventeen years.

24

The Consular Office in
Kingston, Canada, 1878

The last of April [1878] I left Vermont to take up the duties of the consular office at Kingston, Canada. I had but few ideas of what those duties were. President Hayes was the only person who by question or remark gave me the slightest intimation that any special knowledge of the duties would be required. He was one of the advanced men of the times. The majority of people considered that all the knowledge that was necessary was how to get there.

I reached Kingston late in the afternoon. The cabs were a curiosity; I never had seen any like them. I selected one and gave the cabman directions to drive me to a first-class hotel. He left me at the Windsor Hotel on Princess Street. Coming from prohibition Vermont and from the first-class hotels of New Orleans and Washington, I was not pleased with the close proximity of the bar to the clerk's office. There seemed to be no loafing place away from the whisky, so I retired to my room.

In the morning I started out to find the consulate. Colonel [James M.] True was expecting me and said, as I had come to relieve him, he wanted to get rid of the office as soon as he could. Next morning, May 1, I took charge of the consulate. The colonel was a natural product of the spoils system, coming to Kingston, as he said, for the purpose of making what money he could out of the consulate. I do not think he ever let an opportunity escape him, while from ill health or a naturally petulant disposition he had quarreled with both newspapers and the consul general, and in fact seemed to be a man whom all were willing should leave. I could not have been more fortunate in a predecessor, as it required but very little effort to make myself popular.

The city was very interesting; everything looked ancient. The buildings were mostly of stone, heavy and plain, the walks of plank. Martello Tower [was] in front, old Fort Henry looked down upon the city from the east, and a water battery of heavy guns commanded the beautiful landlocked harbor of Kingston.

The city park was surrounded by a high board fence. With some fear that I might be trespassing, I crowded through the narrow gate to discover the reason for such rigid privacy, but found none. To the northwest I found an old burying ground enclosed with a stockade fully fifteen feet high, which, to my chagrin, was locked. This was a great disappointment, as I have a peculiar fancy for visiting old cemeteries. A woman living near the gate, opening her door, called to me that the key was kept at a house some distance to the right of us. I asked her why they kept the gate locked, if the people in there ever got out? She laughed and very rightly shut the door for my impudence.

After a few weeks in the consular office, and at a time when I had found out that there were many things I needed to know which could not be learned from books, Colonel A. D. Shaw, consul at Toronto, who had been in the consular service for many years, came to Kingston and for two or three days gave me the most valuable information referring to consular duties. I shall ever feel very thankful to Colonel Shaw for his valuable kindness. It is more than possible that to his getting me started right may be attributed in a large measure my success as consul.

For a few months my new duties and novel surroundings were sufficiently interesting to keep me contented. When I felt that I was master of my new position, the peace and quiet were almost unbearable. For seventeen years my life had been one of excitement and danger, almost five years in the army and then, in civil life, in more danger than in the army. I had never slept nights without firearms close at hand, [I] never [went] any distance from the house without my revolver, [and] never went into a lighted room while in the country until every curtain was drawn. I then thought that I was enjoying myself, but it was not until near the close of the century that I discovered the nervous exhaustion of such a life.

My property interests at Starlight I had placed in the charge of J. W. Harrison, who went to Louisiana in the 7th Vermont Regiment. He was a man of good education and ability, a brave ex-Federal soldier; but unfortunately for me, he was as reckless with money as with life, and I received nothing from my property after I left it, although under my management it had paid me $8,000 per year. Early in September, 1878, I received notice that Mr. Harrison had been assassinated at Starlight. I immediately sent A. C. Harvey down there to bring away Miss Harrison, who would not leave without bringing the body of her brother.

The Louisiana Democrats thought that they were well rid of me, but there was a large amount of property of which they desired to divest me of by some kind of legal process. Harrison was now out of the way; Joe Pierson secured some imaginary claims, his brother James Pierson acted as his lawyer, and Judge [David] Pierson, another brother,[1] granted the necessary decrees absolutely refusing to allow the cases to go to the United States court, although he admitted that citizens of Vermont owned the property.[2]

The friendliness of the people of Kingston and a final recognition by myself that with my physical disabilities I could not again engage in a life of danger was beginning to make me feel satisfied with the consulate, when the Spanish War broke out. I learned that an old corporal of my company, [now] Lieutenant Colonel [Edwin R.] Shumway of the 1st Massachusetts, was going to the front. It seemed to me a cruel fate to be of no use to my country when she was in war and needing the experience which I had and the physical strength and endurance which once were mine. After a good deal of persuasion, I had asked for an increase in my pension. The order came for my examination. I returned it with the following endorsement: "We are again in war, unknown expenses before the nation, as I am drawing a Government salary, I do not think I shall ask for increase of pension."

1. The Piersons had been White Leaguers and were implicated in the Coushatta Massacre.
2. Twitchell lost Briar Bend in 1881 (*Stafford* v. *Twitchell, Louisiana Annual Reports,* vol. 33, pp. 520–33) and Starlight the following year (*Gillespie* v. *Twitchell,* ibid., vol. 34, pp. 288–300). The heavy legal costs consumed the remainder of his Louisiana holdings.

25

The Spanish Spy and Other Matters

In the afternoon of May 17, 1898, a young man, bright, intelligent-looking, well-dressed, and fully loaded with whisky, abruptly entered the office, advanced to the center of the room, came to attention, saluted, and requested a private interview. He was immediately shown into the private office, where he stood at attention until I was seated and had invited him a second time to take a chair. From his deportment I knew that I had before me a well-drilled English soldier. He said, "I know you very well. I served in the battery in Kingston and always saluted as I met you. I have done a foolish thing, and I want to get out of it; I cannot betray my race. I was drunk or I should not have started. I want to go back to Montreal, but I have drunk up my money and am owing a hotel bill." During this rambling talk he had pulled out of his pocket and placed upon the table a railroad ticket to San Francisco, military discharge and decoration, with a number of other papers, cards, and trinkets. He was carrying so big a load of whisky that I knew he was not very responsible and would be quite likely to take back what he was saying and doing after he was sober.

I rose from my chair, assured him that I was his friend on account of his honorable army service and any mistake which he had made when he was drunk I would have rectified, that I would see to his hotel bill and make arrangements for him to return to Montreal. During this conversation I succeeded in quietly getting him outdoors, requesting him to come back the next day and I would have all arrangements made. As I expected, he was too drunk to remember what he had left in the private office.

Upon a thorough examination the matter was very plain to me that he was an employed spy of the Spanish government. The next forenoon he returned, perfectly sober, and enquired if he had left some papers, a medal, etc., in the office the day before.

I had learned the man's history; he was a good soldier, a first-class artillerist. His wife died before he left Kingston, leaving a little boy and a girl here whom he stopped off to visit on his way to San Francisco. I took him into the private office and informed him that he did leave a number of articles and that many of them he would never get as they were in the possession of the United States government. I then reminded him of his honorable record as a soldier, the death of his wife, his two little children whom he had come to see and who, if he persisted in the course upon which he had started, would ever be burdened with the stain of his actions [and] live to curse their father's name and feel joy and relief at the knowledge of his death; but that he had not gone so far but what the matter could be stopped, his reputation saved, and his children remain free to gain in life the honorable position to which their merits might entitle them. He was soon in tears and decided to undo all the evil which he could.

He had been working in Montreal since his discharge from the battery at Kingston. Soon after the arrival of the Spanish Ministry at that city from Washington, he met a Canadian detective (whose name and card he gave me, with house and office address), a man looking like a Spaniard and speaking that language. They had plenty of money and treated very freely. Finally they made a proposition to him which resulted in the following directions and plans. He was to go to San Francisco or some other point which they might designate, enlist in the American Army, and go to the front. When he was in possession of valuable information and near the Spanish lines, he was to desert or allow himself to be captured by the Spaniards. He was given, in handwriting very neat and plain, the words "Confianza Augustina." These words were to be pronounced to the first officer whom he met, and at the same time he was to ask to be taken to the Spanish general. If this request was not granted, he was to take from his finger the heavy plain silver ring which had been furnished him, call attention to the same words, which were engraved on the inside of the ring, and send it to the Spanish general. He was assured that this would have the desired effect and his request would be granted [and] that he would then be further rewarded either with money or a position in the Spanish Army and perhaps both. He knew there were at least five other men who had such rings, and gave me the names of two. None of them, so far as he knew, were going to San Francisco but to other points. I judged that the Spanish plan was to have their spies separate from each other in different armies. He also gave me the card of a lawyer in Washington. In answer to one of my questions, he said he did not know at first but that he should go through Washington and enlist in the Southern states. I at once secured the complete character, description, and qualifications of the other members of the gang who had served in the battery here. All this information was forwarded to the Department of State.[1]

Montreal was soon filled with American detectives. The attention of the Canadian government was called to the subject, and the headquarters of the Spanish spy system was broken up. I had the satisfaction of seeing in the public press that one of my spies was arrested in Atlanta, another at Tampa, and still another on a man-of-war. The Department of State twice thanked me for the work and sent me a department cypher with authority to draw upon the Secret Service fund for all the money I desired. This was exceedingly satisfactory and made me feel that notwithstanding my physical condition, I had perhaps been able to do as much for the benefit of my nation as I would have done if I had taken the field.

As the railroad refunded the money on the unused ticket to San Francisco, I was able to pay my expenses without drawing one cent on the Secret Service fund. It gave me great satisfaction to think that by this arrangement I had made the gold of the Spanish spy system pay the expenses of its own destruction.

The sudden close of the Spanish War was a world surprise, and no nation was more surprised than the United States. From my experience in the Civil War, coupled with a close observation and study of nations since I entered the consular service, I felt that I was a fairly good judge of such conflicts. I believed that in defense the United States was all-powerful; but an aggressive war, away from home, largely upon the sea, and in an unhealthy climate, I expected would be at least a two-year struggle and would necessi-

---

1. Marshall Harvey Twitchell to Assistant Secretary of State J. B. Moore, May 17, 21, 31, in State Department Records, Record Group 59, National Archives (Microfilm T 472).

tate an immense loss of men and expenditure [of] money. Some of the newspapers of Canada seemed to get much enjoyment by belittling our army [and] navy and in a general way endeavoring to convince their readers of the absolute weakness of the Republic and its insignificant power as compared with the glorious British Empire of which Canada was so proud of being a part. Some of these writers who dipped their pens so deeply in the gall of national envy and abuse must have felt unpleasant upon reading the report of Captain [Arthur Hamilton] Lee, English Attaché of our army at Santiago, when he declared that the American soldier was the superior of any soldier in the world. For this offense in their eyes, he was not punished [but] on the contrary was elected to parliament, where he magnified his grievous offense by declaring that no army except the American army could produce such a combination of bravery and ingenuity as was displayed by the capture of Aguinaldo by Funston.[2] It had only been a few months before this Spanish War that a poor reporter, reporting the lecture of an English officer as actually delivered, said "that it was impossible to defend the frontiers of Canada against the United States." [He] was compelled to say in the next issue that he made a mistake in his report. He told me with tears in his eyes that he had told the truth but that he was compelled to take it back or lose his place. The paper, not the English officer, objected to the report. From the battles, naval and on land at Santiago, the papers gradually became more friendly, and as the war clouds in Europe darkened and Great Britain's isolation became more apparent, they changed still more, and in a year's time they assumed a tone natural to a friendly people of kindred race and common interests.

In the month of October, 1899, the forces of the Orange Free State and Transvaal republic invaded the British colony of Natal. Had the powers been anything like equal, the military strategy of the invasion would have been correct. Under the circumstances these two little republics of half a million people were dependent for their existence upon the good nature of Great Britain. The British Empire dislikes to accept before the nations of the world the position of the oppressor or to pose as a tyrant, but the Boers' policy forced her to assume this role.

2. In March, 1901, Brigadier General Frederick Funston captured Emilio Aguinaldo, leader of the Philippine insurrection against the United States.

Naturally, from the weakness of the British forces in Natal and the complete preparation of the Boers, the invaders were largely successful. Britain was aroused as nothing but defeat could have aroused her. The colonies felt the reverse to the British arms more keenly than the Mother Country. Nations friendly to the republics found themselves in an awkward position, sympathizing with the powers who were aggressors and invaders. No attempt was made by the Boers to conceal their intention of capturing the whole of South Africa.

Canada in two months sent her first contingent of 1,000 men, followed soon after by 2,000 more. When the offer of men was first made by Canada, it was said, and I think with truth, that the Imperial officers thought the best plan would be to scatter the men among the English regiments that they might be taught how to fight. Canadians would not accept this position, and finally they were allowed the great privilege and honor (from the British standpoint) of going under their own officers, none higher in rank than lieutenant colonel.

It is now conceded by a large portion of the British public that their colonial troops of British blood are more effective fighters than those raised in the British Isles. It is strange that after our war of independence and 1812, they should have needed this additional lesson.

During the summer of 1900 English church circles were much interested in the election of a new bishop to this diocese. There was a sharp division between the lay and the clerical members. The balloting was continued for so many days, with repeated adjournments, that it reminded me of the election of United States senators by the Louisiana legislature.

Finally, a very able man by the name of Mills[3] received the election. His consecration was made an affair of great importance. Bishops from the United States and Canada, with lesser lights of the church, were in attendance. Officers of the government, in uniform, were invited. I received an invitation and a verbal request to appear in uniform. As this was a public occasion, and the law allowed me to wear my old uniform, I gratified them by appearing in the dress of a captain of infantry.

3. The Right Reverend William Lennox Mills was chosen Bishop of Kingston in 1900 and Bishop of Ontario the following year.

I gave the subject some thought before I donned the uniform. I reasoned this way: the stronger I can make myself with the influential people of Kingston, the better will I be able to serve my country's interests. I have since discovered that by no little act could I have increased my popularity more. It is a great mistake that our government does not require a uniform for her foreign service as well as for her army and navy, as cities do for their police and large corporations for their employees. It is absurd, as well as weakening to the service, for a rich nation to continue the practices rendered necessary by the early poverty of her people, when her foreign representatives could hardly afford a uniform. I know our government, by meagre salaries and allowances, endeavors to keep its representatives poor; but occasionally a man with sufficient pride, character, and wealth will get a position such that if he were permitted, [he] would dress in a manner suitable to his position. It has occurred more than once that upon public occasions our ministers have been called upon to act as menials on account of their dress, and these mistakes will continue as long as our government compels her representatives to dress as servants.

The personal qualities and life of Queen Victoria were in marked contrast with those of her predecessors. The length of her reign exceeded that of any other British sovereign. She occupied the throne during a period of greater progress and prosperity than any previous fifty years in the world's history; she ascended the throne of Great Britain when it was the only strong English-speaking nation on the face of the globe.

She lived to see a great nation spring from the American colonies of the same kindred race, language, and religion as the Mother Country—a nation so powerful and wealthy that allied with Britain no nation or combination of nations could question their authority. What seemed strange to the world was that the Mother Country and her former rebellious colonies were acting in perfect concert in crowding forward the Christian and commercial civilization of the Anglo-Saxon type. When the electric current flashed to the different parts of the globe the sad intelligence that Queen Victoria's life and reign were ended, the regret and sadness was more general and sincere than was ever known before for earthly sovereign. This was natural in Europe, as she was connected by kinship with most all of the reigning families. In the United States, where there is a natural antagonism towards kings and queens, the grief was general and more sincere. No scandal was ever attached to her name. She always acted for peace [and was] as democratic as could be expected in one occupying a high position by inheritance. A Christian woman, progressive and liberal, an Episcopalian in England, a Presbyterian in Scotland, and the respected sovereign of Jew and Mohammedan. The Episcopal churches in their memorial services attempted to get recognition as the state church of Canada. This was defeated; services were held by all denominations.

I attended the Presbyterian service in St. Andrews Church, the seat in front of the pulpit being draped with the American flag. I was accompanied by the consular clerk, Emmus G. Twitchell,[4] and wore the uniform of my last rank in the United States Army, as allowed by the revised statutes. The interior of the church was heavily draped in mourning, and a large English flag bordered with crape extended over the pulpit. The expressions of sympathy in the United States were so general, that when the civic committee of Kingston arranged for a joint memorial service, I was unanimously selected as one of the speakers. No Episcopal or Catholic clergyman accepted the invitation to be present.

I have just received the following letter. The writer, a warm friend of mine, was adjutant of the regiment during the campaign referred to; consequently, the recommendation must have started from headquarters above regimental.

> Smith, Duncan, Hornbrook & Smith,
> Attorneys At Law
> Indianapolis, Ind., June 5, 1901

My Dear Captain:

Looking through the records of the war as published by the War Department, I found a matter of which I believe I never had any previous knowledge. On May 14th 1865 Genl. R. H. Jackson made a report of the part that the 2nd. Div. 25th Army Corps took in the Appomatox [sic] campaign after he assumed command, and among other recommendations he recommended that Capt. Martin H.

4. Twitchell's son by Henrietta Day.

Twitchell [*sic*] of the 109th U.S.C.I. be awarded a brevet as Major for meritorious services on the campaign from March 27th to April 9th 1865. If I ever had information of this, it had passed out of my mind. I do not know whether you ever heard of it. If not, I am glad you shall hear it now. . . .

Yours Very Truly,
Charles W. Smith[5]

I can think of nothing which any good officer in my place would not leave done under the circumstances with the following exception. The division as I remember it at Hatcher's Run was in regiment column one regiment in rear of the other. It was ordered to deploy to the left into a single line of battle and move forward, each regiment moving to the left flank when it had uncovered. Our regiment, in making the movement, came across an open field where we were exposed to a sharp fire from the enemy's batteries. The colonel was leading the regiment at the extreme left, just entering a wood when we uncovered. There seemed to be none present who observed this fact to give the order "By the right flank." We were exposed to the enemy's fire [and] were getting out of our place. I stepped in front of the line and gave the order "Battalion by the right flank." Officers and men knew this was the proper order, it was promptly obeyed, and the regiment came into its proper position when I gave the command "Halt," and stepped back into my place as captain of Company H.

I never dared to mention this matter even to my friend the adjutant, for I knew quite well the penalties of assuming command and changing direction of the regiment upon the field of battle over the heads of at least two seniors. That I was not put under arrest I have always thought was due to the belief that I was but repeating the orders of some superior officer. The colonel whose ability and bravery were unquestionable must have believed this to have been the case, for that night he selected me to go out in front of the line with him to look over the ground where we were to charge the next day.

5. In the Marshall Harvey Twitchell Papers, Prescott Memorial Library, Louisiana Tech University, Ruston.

Editor's Postscript

The following notice appeared in the *British Whig*, Kingston, Canada, on Monday, August 21, 1905:

Col. Marshall H. Twitchell, United States consul in Kingston for the past twenty-seven years, died at his residence on Wellington street at four o'clock this morning. He never regained consciousness after being stricken with paralysis on Friday morning at half-past seven o'clock. On Sunday morning early, a change for the worse occurred, and the consul sank steadily throughout the day.

Col. Twitchell seemed to be quite well. . . . Quite recently he returned from his annual holiday in Vermont, and appeared in good health. Last Thursday he attended to his office duties as usual, and had a good night's rest. On Friday morning he suddenly collapsed. His death has caused great sorrow among the citizens of Kingston. He has passed to rest after one of the most eventful lives in modern times. For the past forty-five years he served his country in war and peace, and was faithful unto death.

Index